LIVING THE DREAM

7

Seven Key
Principles for Success

BILLY HUFSEY

ISBN-10: 0-578-14899-4
ISBN-13: 978-0-578-14899-1

Dedication

To my parents, Bill & Johanna Hufsey, for teaching me, through the example of their lives, how to live humbly.

Table of Contents

Introduction

Should my life end tonight, I can honestly say I was fortunate enough to live all of my dreams. As a small, sickly kid growing up in Ohio, I dreamed of athletic glory. I was eventually offered collegiate football opportunities and achieved Golden Gloves status as a boxer. In junior high, I used to look at teen magazines and think to myself how cool it would be to appear on their covers one day. Not only did I become a teen idol on a wildly popular television show, I was blessed to have the #1 selling poster in the world. Along the way I also became a national dance champion, starred on a soap opera, toured the world as a musician, and amassed substantial wealth in real estate and banking ventures. I finally came full circle and returned to my original passion for entertainment—this time in a new and even more rewarding capacity. I have been truly blessed.

Despite my dyslexia, and having about a third-grade reading level, I've managed to become a multi-millionaire. I've created/managed/sold/dissolved/developed numerous companies and business entities in varied industries. I own and have owned real estate all over the world. Throughout my life, I have lived my favorite quote multiple times in multiple ways: "Success comes when preparation meets opportunity."

During my brief period living on the streets of Hollywood as a young aspiring actor, I met many colorful characters. One was a homeless man whom I was fascinated to see always reading books. One day I asked him about the material he was reading, and I discovered his story as well.

He shared with me that he was a former college professor. I was surprised to discover that he was a highly educated man. Since I had barely made it out of high school myself, I didn't have a lot of options. In my mind, if you had earned the degrees this man had, any door should be open for him. His situation was completely baffling to me.

He also shared that he found the books he read every day in a dumpster behind the library. What others threw out he voraciously consumed to feed his desire for knowledge. He read something new every day. The pity was that he filled his mind with all of this knowledge, yet he didn't know how to adapt and apply it to himself. Someone so gifted and so smart was missing what I felt was such a simple concept—to try to do whatever it took to get out of the situation he was in and improve his life!

This man was not capable of reinventing himself or being able to picture doing anything other than being a college professor. He felt that there were no other options. In his mind, he believed that the only thing he could do was to teach on that level in that particular setting—a college campus. When he was laid off from his position, he lost everything and was unable to picture doing anything else. That's the key to re-invention: you have to be open to re-imagining your life. Sometimes you have to do something completely outside of your skill set or experience level to sustain yourself until the next door opens. Even when the cards don't fall neatly into place for you to conceptualize an easy transition... *especially* then!

The former professor truly believed that because he couldn't teach at the college level anymore he was done. Meanwhile my mind raced with all of the other potential career options he hadn't explored: librarian, English tutor or literacy volunteer offering lessons for trade with the YMCA or community center in order to get off the streets. Or how about this one: he could have taught young actors in Hollywood!

Being the kind of person I am, with a mind that is constantly maneuvering three steps ahead in every situation to try to benefit my current situation, I asked my new acquaintance if he could help me with techniques to improve my reading skills to help when I went on auditions. Fortunately for me, he was eager to take on a willing student at that moment. The professor taught me to pick out two to three key words within a sentence to derive the meaning of the whole sentence. He also taught me that using the eyes for reading is no different than exercising any other muscle in the body. As with anything new, it took some practice to master this new technique. I am forever grateful for his advice because it's a technique that still serves me well to this day. Bolstered by this game-changer, a few weeks later I was further inspired to re-invent myself to improve my situation and get off the streets.

Several takeaway lessons from that experience have stayed with me for all of these years: always seek more knowledge; be open to learning from anyone, as you never know where the lessons in life will come from; don't judge people solely for their current situation when you don't know their story; and, most importantly, don't become stuck by merely accepting where you are today as your final destination. Never give up hope! When I think back on that time in my life, I always think of the quote: "Shoot for the moon; when you fall short you will land in the stars." Another description that reminds me of the professor is one I heard years later from the great motivational speaker Zig Ziglar: *"The PLOM disease—Poor Little Ole Me."* Strive to never become a PLOM in life.

The most common way people give up their power is by thinking they don't have any.

I was twenty-one when I made the trek out to Hollywood to pursue my dreams in the entertainment industry. In three short years, against overwhelming odds and after plenty of adversity and obstacles, I was firmly walking the path of making my dreams come true. By the time I was twenty-four years old I had made my first million. It's just that simple: If you believe you can achieve your dreams—you can. I know because it happened to me. We must believe that we are gifted and meant for something, and that this thing, at whatever cost, must be attained.

After three decades in Hollywood, I am happy, healthy and still living my dreams every day. But at this point in my life my mission has changed. Now my goal is to help others live their own dreams. I want everyone to know what it feels like to turn fantasy into reality. After my aspirations of becoming a professional athlete were shattered I shifted my dream to show business. Your dreams may perhaps be a career in the business world, achieving an athletic or fitness goal, attaining a degree in a specialized field, earning a certain salary, or just lie in the realm of strengthening and improving your personal relationships. I have written this book because I want to help you attain your goals. These days, I am *giving* to make a living. There's no better feeling than helping others achieve true success… whatever their own personal definition of that might be!

There are, of course, numerous books already on the market about how to become successful, build wealth or achieve your heart's desire. I actually recommend many during speaking engagements. The true key to success, though, is to not only *read* the information contained in these published works but to *take ownership* of that information and apply the principles in your everyday life. Not every concept in every book, including this one, will work for or apply to all people. You have to be able to critically examine the material and determine what will inspire and spur you on to making some changes in your own life.

So…why this particular book? Thirty-some years into it, I'm still thriving in one of the toughest businesses in the world. I have encapsulated my hard-earned lessons and very best advice into seven directives that, when followed faithfully, cannot fail to help you find your own version of success. Don't just take my word for it. Over the years I've encountered every kind of person in every circumstance imaginable. I've encouraged everyone from Carol Burnett to Asia Monet Ray over the years … and some of my friends will share their own very individual stories of how these concepts worked for them.

Here are my keys for success:

Manage your Mind
Embrace your Authentic Self
Overcome Adversity
Plan and Prepare
Ready for Reinvention
Persevere
Nurture your Spirit

All of the above are proven entities that I have used to achieve every one of my various dreams. As we go through the book, we will discuss each of these concepts in much greater detail.

This book is an extension of the work I hold so dear to my heart, which is helping others. In short, this book is my labor of love. It is about how I learned to live the days of my life after I discovered I wasn't actually going to live forever. Remember: "*If it is to be, it is up to me*" translates to the reality that you must do more than read books. *You* have to do the work. *You* must invest the time. *You* must dedicate your actions, thoughts and words toward achieving your own goals, dreams and passions. I am here to get you up and on your feet. Get motivated! Stay on your hustle! You don't fail until you quit. Your life is your message to the world. Make it inspiring!

Photo by: Barbara Froelich

Billy Hufsey

In the Beginning

"God can always dream a bigger dream for you than you can dream for yourself."

— Oprah Winfrey

Let's get started on the most important journey of your life—the one that ends with you achieving your personal best and maximizing your success! Personal power comes from within, and tapping into its source is very attainable for anyone. You *are* good enough to achieve success. Never forget that. As my father used to say, "Everyone puts their pants on the same—one leg at a time. No one is any better than you."

What we can or cannot do, what we consider possible or impossible, is rarely a function of our true capability. It is more likely a function of our beliefs about who we are.

BILLY AND HIS DAD, BILL HUFSEY, SR. DECEMBER 2013

Because my dad was a very popular and well-liked man, high expectations were placed on the Hufsey kids in Brook Park, Ohio, where I grew up. My two sisters and I couldn't do anything without our parents finding out. Dad was the town's recreation director—a political position—and in that capacity he knew everyone. Everyone in town knew us as well.

My dad had no formal education, not even a high school diploma, when he signed up to fight for our country during World War II. He served in the Pacific before returning home. He started loading trucks and worked his way up the ladder working for the city of Brook Park in various different departments. Eventually, he landed his dream job—one typically only given to those with college degrees. In ten years he had no less than three ball fields named after him: Hufsey 1, 2, & 3. He transformed the department in our small community into one of the top ten best recreation programs in the state of Ohio.

When I was five years old I contracted rheumatic fever. My bout with this disease was compounded by the fact that I am allergic to penicillin. Back in 1963, there weren't a lot of options on how to treat such a serious infection raging through my small body. For those who may not know what rheumatic fever is, here's the official definition according to dictionary.com:

rheumatic fever
noun; Pathology

A serious disease, associated with streptococcal infections, usually affecting children, characterized by fever, swelling and pain in the joints, sore throat and cardiac involvement.

Even those who survive the actual fever and fight off the infection face complications. Rheumatic fever often causes permanent injury to the heart, ranging from damage to the valves all the way up to complete heart failure. The reality is that very few people who have had rheumatic fever as a young child live past their thirties. Okay, so I can't swear that that last statement is 100% medically factual. Ironically, given my passionate interest in studying medicine, I've never chosen to research that particular statistic myself. However, that's what I was told all my life growing up. Back then there were plenty of well-known examples that others were constantly pointing out to me.

One example of someone famous with rheumatic fever dying young was Bobby Darin, the singer, songwriter and actor best known for his hit songs *Splish Splash, Dream Lover, Mack the Knife,* and *Beyond the Sea.* He died at the age of 37 following a heart operation in Los Angeles. Those closest to me know how thankful I am every day just to wake up and be alive. I truly appreciate the gift that each day brings in and of itself. I am grateful that I am still here and doing well; because statistically, I shouldn't be alive today to share my story. The fact that I am fifty-five years old and still living my dreams amazes me every day.

However, this is still a part my everyday reality. I have scar tissue. I have mitral prolapsed valves. I have an enlarged heart. I have cardiovascular disease. However and here's the most important part of my reality: *Rheumatic fever and its permanent ill effects do not have me.* What could have been the greatest setback or obstacle in my life has instead shaped my destiny in a positive way—because I chose to not let it define me. More importantly, at the tender age of five, my mother chose to not let my heart issues define me or what I would accomplish in my life.

After surviving rheumatic fever I got sick very easily. I endured countless sore throats, many minor illnesses and even scarlet fever. I had setback after setback with my health. I actually appeared to stop growing in the fifth grade and didn't start growing significantly again until around the tenth grade. My health challenges profoundly hindered my development during my formative school years. Not to mention my learning challenges caused by dyslexia.

In grade school I was bullied briefly for being small and was labeled "dumb" due to my dyslexia. Nowadays dyslexia can be worked around; parents and teachers know how to handle it. Back then, it was just an embarrassment that I couldn't read or do the things that were so simple for my peers. There was very little understanding and no official diagnosis of this condition. It wasn't even recognized as a condition. I always felt like the underdog and like I was never good enough. I certainly never felt smart enough to be successful at pursuing my dreams.

I knew I wasn't dumb even though I didn't always get the best grades in class. I eventually realized that I had to listen hard and remember what the teachers said in class to acquire the information they were teaching. I also knew I would always have to work much harder than the other students to train my eyes and brain how to process written words better, as reading would never come easily to me.

These were difficult years for me. "Shrimp" and "dumb" were labels others had put on me. Due to my mother's unwavering faith in what I could accomplish in my life, I knew I was ultimately the only one who could choose what labels I wanted to allow to be placed on myself. My mom was the one who insisted that I stand up for myself. Even if I took a whooping, I had to learn to stand my ground. With the confidence of my mom believing in me, I finally did stand up for myself, and that was the last time I was bullied. Life is too short to allow others to label you or dictate how you're going to live your life.

> One isn't necessarily born with courage, but one is born with potential. Without courage, we cannot practice any other virtue with consistency. We can't be kind, true, merciful, generous, or honest.

My mom provided the best advice and greatest encouragement to me, always. She frequently exhorted, Never give up! Never stop! There's always a way, you just might not have discovered it yet. Mom always told me to shoot for eternity. She was a great inspiration all of my life and a key factor in all the successes I have achieved. I think she was a key to my father's success as well because she was so supportive to his career and the achievement of his dreams.

BILLY AND HIS MOM - IN CALIFORNIA ON HIS HARLEY

I count myself fortunate to have had many strong female influences in my life: sisters, cousins and aunties. My Aunt Hilly was like a second mother to me; and with a seven and nine-year age gap between me and my sisters, it sometimes felt like I was mothered by both sisters and all of their friends as well. Not to mention my four female cousins. It turns out this was the best thing in the world for me, because I learned early on how the other half of the population works, thinks and feels. This knowledge would prove very valuable later in life.

Being raised around so many females helped me get in touch with my sensitive side. It certainly helped me become a better actor, because I am more in touch with my emotions and can be more empathetic. Still, in many ways I believe women are a lot stronger than men; I learned from being surrounded by them that they have many strengths that men do not. So instead of rebelling against girls, I chose to learn from them.

Meanwhile, the example provided by my dad taught me not only to have a spirit of service to our community, but also showed me that the path to achieving a dream wasn't necessarily always a straight line. He had certainly demonstrated that anything was possible if you held tight to your dreams. Dad never made much money, but he understood passion—that was very, very important and he made sure I knew it.

When I was in junior high, my dad was laid off from his job for political reasons. I learned from watching him go from a white-collar to a blue-collar job about tenacity and the do-whatever-it-takes mentality required to survive adversity and tough times financially. I also learned how family could pull together and work hard to survive rough patches. I came to a couple of very valuable realizations early in life: Because there were things I wanted that my parents couldn't pay for, I would have to find ways of getting them for myself; and the importance of remaining flexible and willing to re-invent myself to achieve goals.

The most important thing you can do to achieve your goals is to make sure that as soon as you set them down, you immediately begin to create momentum. The most important rules I ever adopted to help me achieve my goals were to first write down the goal, and then to never leave the site of setting a goal without first taking some form of positive action toward its attainment.

The process of looking back and pulling together old stories and past experiences to compile this book put me in quite a self-reflective mode. One thing that is quite clear, however, is that my parents laid a strong foundation for my future success. Many of the rules I would live by are a credit to them.

CHAPTER ONE

Manage Your Mind

"Whether you think you can or think you can't—you're right."
—Henry Ford

Never underestimate the power of your mind. It is the single most powerful tool within your means to use and control in order to achieve dreams and goals. When you believe something, your mind finds ways to achieve, and you'll start thinking constructively.

Start by resolving to never again use the word *impossible.* Impossible is a failure word and will set your mind to react in a way to prove you are right. You have to believe it can be, whatever your "it" is that you want to achieve. Be open and receptive to new ideas. Be open and progressive in your thinking. Never regress, as there is no place for regression in positive thinking. The past cannot be changed, but the future is yours if you believe it can be.

We must believe we are destined for something, and that this thing, at whatever cost, must be attained.

Once you have an idea, believe in it and build the confidence to proceed with turning your idea into reality. Don't let it escape! Write your ideas down, review them daily and cultivate them in your mind. Believe these ideas can become reality. Stretch your mind and get stimulation by associating with people who can help you think through the new ideas. Brainstorm ways to accomplish your goals and dreams. Then formulate a concrete goal and concise plan for achieving that goal!

Pastor Joel Osteen stated this point best when he said, "Whatever follows '*I am....*' will always find you." So if you say, for example, "I am fat, lazy and tired," guess what's going to find you. You will feel and be fat, lazy and tired. But if you turn your thoughts around and say, "I am healthy, energized and looking forward to getting my second wind to keep going," what do you think will happen? You will feel healthy, energized and have enough energy to get through your day.

Wouldn't you prefer to control your thoughts so they will provide positive outcome and the results you desire? I sure do!

> I challenge you to make your life a masterpiece. I challenge you to join the ranks of those people, who live what they teach, who walk their talk.

No man is an island. Establish yourself as a team player: as a finger you are a weak entity; together you can make a fist that is a power punch to success.

Pay close attention to your environment and everyone who surrounds you in your work and personal lives. Study each of these various people and how they approach their daily activities as well as how they respond to you and others. Ask yourself some difficult questions about these particular people; be willing to honestly evaluate their attitudes vs. their level of personal successes. Observe what they are telling you about themselves through their words and actions. By listening critically, you will learn all you need to know about a person's way of thinking by evaluating their communications.

Once you've made these assessments, you must then ask yourself who you want to surround yourself with to help you achieve your dreams and goals. Those who will be supportive and help lift you up to attain your dreams, or those who bring you down with their negativity and present roadblocks in the path to your success? The people you choose to associate with daily have a tremendous impact on your mental outlook, which in turn affects your ability to achieve success in every aspect of your life. Conversely, the attitudes you convey to the people in your life have a similar impact on them. Evaluate your own mental attitude honestly. Ask yourself: are you a positive influence on others?

Many popular motivational books on the market today classify a person's communication style in one of two ways: as being either *'Small'* or *'Big.'* Small people monopolize conversations by talking; big people monopolize by listening. The ideal style is an effective balance of the two. Mix with people of different occupational and social interests to get even better ideas on ways for you to achieve your best personal success. Critically analyzing and studying the people around you is one of the best ways to help you establish your own parameters for changing your way of thinking and interactions with those around you every day.

Utilizing Affirmations to Change Your Subconscious

You are in control of you... and you can be where you want to be. You are enough to accomplish the dreams and goals you set for yourself. Believe this to be true above all else: *You are enough.* Repeat that to yourself as an important early step toward changing your way of thinking.

Affirmations are a highly effective tool to reprogram your subconscious. It's one way to change your inner dialogue to achieve the dreams and success you desire. Everyone has an inner dialog consisting of all of the things they have ever heard or been told about themselves by others throughout the course of their life—whether they are true or not.

Throughout the formative years of our early development we hear many things about ourselves from our parents, grandparents, siblings, extended family members and caretakers. These are the first people who tell us what they see us to be. That's not to say they are telling us *who* we truly are or who we will eventually become; however, all too often these are the first people to place labels and limitations on us, thereby shaping our subconscious perceptions of ourselves. Not every person in our family or our lives will be positive or encouraging. Oftentimes our most damaging self-perceptions come from words and labels from the people who love us the most, said without conscious malicious intent. Sadly, at other times, harsh words and labels are the unfortunate intent.

> There are no classes in life for beginners;
> right away you are always asked to deal
> with what is most difficult.

When we start school and experience social interactions with our peers we tend to have more labels placed on us by others: the jock, the bookworm, the nerd, the teacher's pet. These labels enable others to place us in categories that limit our own personal achievements and dreams. Who's to say that the most talented athlete and jock in school isn't also an amazing artist who derives just as much soul fulfillment and joy in creating a beautiful sculpture as he does from scoring touchdowns?

The inner dialogue in your mind has a tremendously powerful effect on shaping your picture of yourself, thereby either limiting or enhancing what you can achieve in your life. If you believe only what others have said about you, you will never reach your highest truth and potential of what you can become. No one knows you—your dreams, goals, wishes and desires—better than you. You wouldn't have your individual dreams, goals, wishes and desires inside you without the ability to make them a reality. Many of us need a little help in reprogramming our inner dialogue to see past the limiting labels other have placed on us. This is where affirmations come in as an amazing tool to help undo any negative images we can carry of ourselves.

Change the way you look at things
and the things you look at change.

There are numerous books on the market and articles on the internet that talk about affirmations. They list sample affirmations and help you formulate specific affirmations you can write that will apply to your own life and goals. You don't even have to acknowledge any negative labels that might have been said about you, or even know exactly what you want to achieve. However, it is imperative that negative words are NOT a part of your affirmations. The primary objective of an affirmation is to replace negative internal dialog with only positive words, thoughts and ideas to reprogram your subconscious.

A well-crafted affirmation does not reflect your current reality! Remember that whatever you affirm, you will manifest in your life. When you can harness the power of your subconscious mind, you have the power and ability to change your world in remarkable ways. I was told I would never make it as a performer. However, in the picture I could clearly see of myself, I had made it. I would make it. I did make it!

The more you see yourself as what you'd like to become, and act as if what you want is already there, the more you'll activate those dormant forces that will collaborate to transform your dream into your reality.

I am sure everyone has heard of corporations and businesses having a mission statement. I am equally sure you haven't heard of many individuals doing the same for themselves personally. I promise you that it is one of the best ways to focus your energy, efforts and actions in the right direction. If you don't write your goals down, how can you ever truly formulate a realistic plan to achieve them?

The way to create a personal mission statement is to continue answering questions about yourself—where you've been, where you want to go. Here are a few more questions to get you started:

- How do you envision your ideal life?
- What dreams do you want to achieve?
- What changes do you want or need to implement?
- What is your passion?

(If you're not sure, ask yourself what the one thing is that you could do all day long; losing all track of time while you do it, because that one thing makes your heart smile and your soul feel alive? That's your passion.)

- When you were a little kid, what did you want to be when you grew up?
- What goals have you set for yourself? Your life?
- What is the time frame for achieving your goals?
- What are the benefits of the goals that you desire?

Passion is a feeling that tells you: this is the right thing to do. Nothing can stand in my way. It doesn't matter what anyone else says. This feeling is so good that it cannot be ignored. I'm going to follow my bliss and act upon this glorious sensation of joy.

These questions should help you identify what you define as your dream for success and the desired goals to take you there. With that established, you can formulate a personal mission statement to start developing plans to make your dreams come true. Start a goal diary. There is tremendous power in being able to visualize what you want to achieve once you commit your thoughts and dreams to paper. As scary as it is to actually write your specific dreams and goals down for fear of failing to achieve them, it is infinitely scarier to never write them down at all. To never have the guts to formulate a plan at all. Remember: The risk is not in taking the risk and failing—the risk is never taking the risk at all.

When you temporarily run aground, remember that there are no failures in life. There are only results. Consider the adage: success is the result of good judgment; good judgment is the result of experience; and experience is often the result of bad judgment.

During this process it is also imperative to focus on the benefits of your goals as opposed to focusing on the obstacles or difficulties in achieving our goals. Consider, for example, the person who talks themselves out of going back to college to complete their degree because it will take ten years or costs too much. The real question to ask is: Where will you be ten years from now if you don't have the degree? What will that cost you? Or consider the person who argues that if they stop smoking they will gain weight. In this case the real questions are what do you gain if you continue to smoke, and what do you stand to lose?

The key to creating a truly successful mission statement is to change your way of thinking: change your perceptions of how you look at life, where you want to go, what you want to achieve and how you are going to get there. The old adage *"perception is reality"* is so very true. What are your perceptions? Your realities? The key is to remember that if you find something you love to do for a living, then you will never work a day in your life.

Your current objective:

- Create a Personal Mission statement,
- Set your goal(s),
- Develop a plan of action,
- See yourself successful, and then work backwards to get there.

Here are some examples of Personal Mission Statements that should help jumpstart your journey toward creating your own:

- To remember where I've been and where I will go while maintaining true to the dreams of my heart, true to the people in my life who offer kindness and support while walking away from anything that's not fully supportive of my dreams.
- To joyously live each day to its fullest, striving for inner peace while remaining open and positive to new experiences and knowledge all while maintaining razor-like determined focus toward the achievement of the passions and dreams of my heart.
- To nurture and develop the talents and aspirations unique to my journey while maintaining true to the core character values important in life: Honor, integrity, honesty, loyalty and perseverance. To inspire others daily by being the positive influence I value so that I can lead by example.

A positive attitude will attract opportunity.

Your mind can carry you to success or produce total failure. It is all in what you think. Think your way to where you want to be. During this process you will need to manage and control your environment. Your brain will reflect what your environment feeds it. Our habits and mannerisms, as well as our taste in literature, music, clothing and food tend to be dictated by the places we hang out in and the people we hang out with. Bearing this in mind, you need to be aware of these environmental influences and avoid negative and distasteful situations and people.

If you want to be successful, find someone who has achieved the results you want and copy what they do, and you'll achieve the same.

Spending time with people who have achieved success and practicing positive thinking raises our own level of success. It is a common belief amongst professionals that while we are all products of our environment, which may have been circumstantially negative in early life, we are capable of refusing to allow any negative early experiences to affect our chances for success. We recondition ourselves to understand suppressive and negative forces and outthink them by replacing them with positive, responsible thinking and beliefs.

If you are to be, you must begin by assuming responsibility. You alone are responsible for every moment of your life, for every one of your acts.

I hope you are beginning to realize just how powerful your mind can be in your journey toward achieving your highest personal success. You and you alone can positively affect not only your life but the lives of those around you every day....through the simple power of maintaining a positive mental attitude.

Each and every day, when you wake up in the morning you make a choice if you are going to have a good day or a bad day. Each and every moment of that day you make hundreds of split-second decisions of how you will react to what is going on around you. At work, at home, just standing in line at the grocery store—you have hundreds of choices every day as to how you are going to deal with your daily circumstances. Do you smile and say hello when you pass a stranger? Or do you hold your head down and look at the floor, avoiding eye contact as you pass someone by? You may not even realize it, but you are actually making a choice—not consciously—about your attitude and how you are going to deal with what is going on around you.

Here's a quick, easy exercise for you to try that will demonstrate what I am trying to convey: Stand up, back straight and shoulders back, good posture, head held high with a smile on your face for two minutes (and I hope you know NOT to lock your knees or you're going to have a different problem altogether.) How do you feel? Do you feel happy or sad? Positive or negative? Now stand with your shoulders slumped over, looking down with a scowl on your face and hold the position for two minutes. (Remember—no knee-locking!) How do you feel now? Positive… or negative? Did you notice a difference?

It is a scientific fact that if every muscle in your body is in a positive position, you cannot be in a negative mood. And the reverse is true as well. What does that tell us? It tells me that we have the power to control our moods and how we feel each and every day. If you have that kind of mental power, why not utilize it in a purposeful and conscious way to be positive? Don't you want to leave a positive impression on those you encounter? Why not spread some happiness and positivity as you go throughout your day… and life? What a simple, pure gift you can give to yourself and to others every day… and best of all: It's free!

Being in a good frame of mind helps
keep one in the picture of health.

Here's another way to think of our mind and how it works: Every thought is a seed. When you think of it from that perspective, you then can ask yourself: what do you want to *harvest* in your life? If you can answer that question, then you'll know what kinds of seeds you need to plant in your life to harvest the results you desire. And all of that is freely within your power to control.

Imagine. Visualize. Achieve.

The following are a few quotes that I believe can have a profound impact to shape your personal, positive mental attitude, image and perceptions of yourself and what you can achieve:

"As one thinketh in his heart, so is he."

~ The prophet David

"Great men are those who see that thoughts rule the world."

~ Ralph Waldo Emerson

"The mind is its own place and in itself can make a heaven of hell or a hell of heaven."

~ from Milton's *'Paradise Lost'*

"'There is nothing either good or bad except that thinking makes it so."

~ William Shakespeare

All the above simply state that if you can *Imagine it ... Visualize it...* truly *Envision* yourself doing it.... then you can make it happen. So the obvious conclusion then is to *Imagine* and *Visualize* and *Envision* positive and LARGER THAN LIFE (or anyone else's) thoughts to proceed to achieve your personal success: emotional, financial, or anything you desire or define as success for you in your life.

Be enthusiastic!

No one else can live your life except for you. And no one else knows the dreams, goals and desires of your heart better than you. So you are the only one responsible for your own achievements, for your own successes and your own dream fulfillment. That's not to say you are an island and can achieve all of your goals without assistance from others along the way. However, if you aren't working the hardest for your own personal goal fulfillment, how can you expect others to give you their best to help you along your journey?

To be successful, you have to see yourself successful. You have to see yourself accomplishing whatever your "it" is. Once you can visualize yourself as you want to be or who you want to become you have to work backwards to get there with the tenacity and fortitude to see it through.

When you know where you're going, the world comes together to help you get where you want to go. The world changes for you. When you breathe life into your goals and dreams by writing them down on paper and formulating a plan to achieve them, you set in motion a series of events that allows the universe to help you accomplish your goals, dreams and desires. You change your mind-set to allow your aspirations to become a reality. When you change your picture you will change your world.

Before success comes in any one's life, he/she is sure to meet with much temporary defeat and, perhaps, some failures. When defeat overtakes a person, the easiest and most logical thing to do is quit. That is exactly what the majority of people do. Defeat is not the worst of failures. Not to have ever tried is the true failure.

Success is never final. Failure is never fatal.
Courage is what counts.

JAMES MENCINI I grew up here in Brook Park, Ohio; a local boy just like Billy. I've known him since we were kids. In high school we both took summer jobs coaching little kids' baseball. He, of course, took off to LA after high school; meanwhile I stayed and took a job for the city. As a matter of fact, I worked for Billy's dad for a short while. His father is a wonderful man and a great boss, who played a major role in turning our village of Brook Park into an official city.

After years of working city jobs, next thing you know I became a coach. For many years I was an assistant; starting in the year 2000 I took on basketball as well as football and baseball. I became the head coach of four teams: two girls' teams and two boys' teams. I've had some great success and quite a few winning seasons since then. What I'm really proud of is that I believe I have built good solid programs here for kids that emphasize character. If you play for me, you will learn a lot about the sport, but also about how to live a good life.

Billy and I grew up in Ward 3, but as an adult I wound up building a house in Ward 2 so that's the district I represent now as a city councilman. No one ran against me, and I'd like to think that has something to do with my good reputation as a coach and educator. I want to look ahead, contribute to my city going forward and making it the best place possible for us all to live. Billy's family was a big part of instilling these values in me in my early years.

Both Billy's parents were active in many committees and organizations, and of course his dad was the Recreation Director for many years. I really absorbed many lessons about civic responsibility from his family. They also hammered home the fact that every man and every woman is created equal. You are never better than the guy next door, and you're not that far away from the guy under the bridge. Their compassion and caring for all members of our community truly inspired me.

Billy, of course, had a huge hit with his role on FAME. He was really famous; every head would turn when he walked into a place when he was home for the weekends. Billy was always great when people approached him wanting autographs or just to talk; he told me, "They feel like they know me from watching me on TV." He was always very gracious. To this day people still inquire about him. . . just today someone asked what my old friend Billy Hufsey was up to.

One night back in the eighties the two of us were out. This was right at the peak of his fame while starring on TV as Christopher Donlon. We were in a bar and as usual Billy had a bunch of girls around him. He was telling a story, waving his arms around, talking very animatedly and making all the girls giggle. Suddenly a young woman broke into the conversation, walking right up to Billy and interrupting. She was quite bold. "See my friend over there?" she pointed to a booth in the back, where another girl was sitting alone. "She just found out her mother has cancer. It came as a real shock, the cancer is very aggressive and her mom is still so young; she's just devastated."

"Really?" Billy said. This immediately touched his heart, given how close he was to his own mother.

"Yes, I made her come out tonight, trying to cheer her up. She is such a big fan of yours. If you have some time later tonight, maybe you could come by the table and just say hi to her."

Billy and I looked over at the girl, who was staring down at the table looking downcast. "Sure," he said, and smiled at all the girls. "Finish your drinks, I'll be back soon," he told us all, and accompanied the woman back to her table. He slid right into their booth and stayed for an hour, talking intently with the girl, holding her hand, handing her napkins when she cried, listening to every word, even making her laugh a few times. He politely turned away other fans who tried to approach him at the booth. He was intent upon cheering this girl up.

This is a perfect example of the kind of young man he was, and remains to this very day. Those are the kind of values I hope to instill in the kids I coach now. You help others in their time of need, and others will help you, I tell them. That's how this world goes around. Now, society has changed a great deal since Billy and I were growing up, and the world has certainly changed. But Billy and his family inspired me to always strive to be a giving and compassionate person. The kindness in Billy's heart comes from his mom, while his intense drive and focus on business comes from his dad. His mother had a very soft heart and a great love for others, which is alive and well in her son.

Over the years we always kept in touch... he was the Hollywood star, I was the hometown boy back in Ohio. He showed me the world: New York, LA, Vegas... we've traveled all over together. He's shared a great deal of his life with me and been a true friend. Billy's a very driven, passionate guy. I've seen him handle people when he was at the very top of the mountain, I've seen him when he was at the bottom. He has always been and remains the same person.

Dare to be different, I tell my kids. I love the ones who don't follow the group, who blaze their own path, who march to the beat of their own drummer. That's the kind of kid Billy was, and I do my best to nurture that kind of kid now. At this point in our lives Billy and I are both passionate about coaching and helping kids. The most difficult—and most rewarding—thing I've ever done in my life is to coach teenage girls. I'm in my fourteenth year now and have gone to two weddings already this year. These girls are all like daughters to me... just as I know Billy's kids are to him. I am a lucky man to have the chance to share my passion as well as my values with the next generation. Just like my friend Billy Hufsey.

CHAPTER TWO

Overcome Adversity

"Whenever we look upon this earth, the opportunities take shape within the problems."

—Nelson A. Rockefeller

When I share my life experiences in this book, I do not list any of my accomplishments to brag. Quite the opposite! The point I want to make is that none of these things came easily. Problems, obstacles, and bumps in the road... everyone faces them. The important thing is that I overcame mine. I am here as living proof that you can overcome yours as well!

Medical technology and research has come a long way since I contracted rheumatic fever fifty years ago. I can't do anything about the permanent damage that was done to my heart. I can, however, do something about the rest of my body that is within my power to control. I can also keep my mind sharp to maneuver and manage whatever obstacles and challenges may come my way. I strive every day to maintain peak health through cardio exercise, eating for optimal health for my body and blood type, as well as recognizing my personal limits for how hard I can push myself and when I need to hold back. I have a tendency to get sick very easily, which has caused me to be what some might refer to as a germ-a-phobe. I can literally go from sniffles in the morning to needing to be checked into the hospital by evening if I don't stay in tune with my body and what it needs to stay healthy each day. That's my personal reality—everyone's reality is different. But in acknowledging this reality and knowing the parameters I have to work in each day, I maximize the positives in my life that are within my power to change and control every day.

I love the quote that Good Morning America anchor Robin Roberts frequently utters and attributes to her own tenacious mother: "Make your mess your message." Each and every one of us has our own challenges and obstacles to overcome. Our goal in life should not only be to overcome what stands in the way to our success but to also empower and uplift others to overcoming their challenges and obstacles.

Adversity is the mother of progress.

One of my earliest dreams was to play high school football. Like most little boys, I wanted to run into the end zone, scoring the winning touchdown for my team at the last minute, with all of the fans in the bleachers standing and cheering my name. I wanted to be the hero. Isn't that what most little boys who play football dream about?

Given my health challenges, that goal did seem a bit far-fetched on the surface. Although I did play football—in pee-wee ball, bantam leagues and in junior high—I was much too small to physically contribute to the team and play at the competitive level needed for success at the high school level. Or so I thought.

My mom understood first-hand my desire to achieve success as an athlete, because she was one herself. She played baseball and volleyball and was also an avid golfer and bowler. She cheered me on as I redirected my athletic aspirations toward boxing, which developed my physical skills and mental acuity. In the ring I learned to trust myself, my own physical strength and the ability to think on my feet. Additionally, during these years I spent many hours in the gym building my physical muscle strength.

I had also been bowling since the age of eight. Though I was passionate about boxing and football, I discovered I had a real knack for bowling. The difference between the three sports is the subtlety of focus. I loved the challenge of getting in my head, approaching the foul line, and releasing the ball as smoothly as I could, with just the right amount of speed and lift of the fingers as I let the ball go. Bowling is a surprisingly creative and complex sport; one I truly believe sparked my creative development process. Instead of a team sport, my success was wholly dependent of my own skills and abilities. The fluidity, focus and concentration I honed bowling are all key skills that I am grateful I developed early. At the age of twelve I became Ohio's state bowling champ!

Typical kids my age—junior high—just wanted something simple like a bike. I, on the other hand, was obsessed with a new goal—becoming a black belt in karate. Inconveniently I wanted this just as my dad was laid off from his job for political reasons. I negotiated with the owner of the local karate studio to clean their floors and windows in exchange for free classes. During this time I also had a paper route, built a small landscaping company and negotiated with local insurance companies to pass out flyers advertising their businesses. The entrepreneurial spirit was alive and thriving in my young world. And this mentality has continued throughout my life and career.

I learned a long time ago that winners do what losers won't. I knew I had to work harder, smarter and more strategically to overcome my shortcomings of having dyslexia, not being born to a family of privilege and facing major health challenges early in life. I knew no one was going to hand me an opportunity that I had to go out there and create opportunities for myself, earning my way to where I wanted to be.

Obstacles are only negatives when we allow them to be. The path to success isn't always the most obvious direct path. Sometimes it takes us a few tries, taking a new path or finding a new way of perceiving the obstacle standing in the way of whatever we desire. Sometimes an obstacle can cause us to go in an entirely different direction in our lives before we are able to come back to the original dream and achieve it—in addition to the other successes we found along the way.

> Though no one can go back and make a brand-new start, anyone can start from now and make a brand-new ending.

As a kid I sometimes felt like I could never live up to my father's expectations or the stories he used to tell about people who had excelled—in sports, for example. I didn't let it affect me negatively, as it drove me to excel, even though I wasn't blessed with the specific gifts that others were born with.

Although I was still smaller than most players, I wasn't about to let go of my dream. When I tried out for the football team in my senior year of high school I wanted the spot of tight end over a player who was 6'5" and 250 pounds—when I was merely 5'11" and weighed only 147 pounds. Unfortunately for me, the rule of thumb for seniors was that you had to have played in your junior year to even make the team, let alone make the starting lineup. I managed to succeed in making the team—only to be relegated to riding the bench.

The coach made me sit out the first three games of the season. I had worked so hard for so long and legitimately earned a spot on the team, only to be forced to sit and watch everyone else do what I wanted to do from a front-row seat on the field. I was so angry and frustrated I wanted to walk away from it all.

The Monday after that third miserable game sitting on the bench, I skipped afternoon practice. A buddy of mine came by the house to pick up my equipment. He might as well have it, because I fully intended to leave the team. My mom was puzzled to see him heading toward the door carrying all of my football equipment. She wasn't having any of that! Mom flat-out refused to let me quit. She told my buddy to go back and tell the coach that I would be there the next day after school. I was there—and I was miserable with the high intensity practice and extra drills. I had to endure extra cardio and physically exhausting drills all week to regain my place back on the team.

BILLY AND HIS MOMA, JOHANNA HUFSEY

That Friday evening found me in what seemed to be my permanent place on the team—holding down the bench. The weather was miserable, with rain pouring down the entire game. My parents, as always, sat loyally in the stands in the downpour. The clock showed thirty seconds left in the game when the coach approached me. He wanted to put me in! I had one play. From the moment I ran onto the field the scene unfolded like a perfectly scripted Hollywood movie. I had only one guy to hit. I took that one chance and rushed at that guy with everything I had in me. I hit the other player so hard he flew one way as I went the other. We left a hole big enough for the running back to make a 63-yard run down the field—only to cramp up and fall two yards from the end zone.

We may not have scored on that play, but I had managed to score a permanent starting position on the team. I started in every football game after that, and was even offered opportunities to play ball at the collegiate level, but that was not to be. My career aspirations would soon take a very different turn; but more on that later. For now, let me say that these events set the precedent for how I live my life every day and approach all obstacles that come my way.

This is the perfect example of how an obstacle in my life—my size—didn't stop me from accomplishing my dreams. I simply redirected my energies to accomplish something else that later led to my achievement of my original dream. I have my mom to thank for teaching me this valuable lesson. When I was ready to quit, she wouldn't let me. She told me I must always finish what I started. This event was also a great testament to my mother's tenacity and her belief in her children to succeed and accomplish their dreams.

Surmounting difficulty is the crucible that forms character.

Sure there are obstacles—or perceived obstacles—that stand in the way of achieving your Personal Mission Statement. We all face numerous obstacles in our path every day. Some are big and some are small; some are known and others are unpleasant surprises along the way. We must constantly overcome something—often many things. That's just life. If we identify the obstacles we do know, then we can formulate ways of overcoming them. That way when the expected challenges arise, we don't feel overwhelmed. We are prepared with a plan to overcome that obstacle.

A key element of obstacle identification is to remember that there is a distinct difference between a *condition* and a *problem.* An example of a *condition* is being born without a limb. A *problem* arises when you allow that particular birth defect to define your own (or another's) abilities or what they are capable of achieving. A condition can be identified and worked around. A problem is a complete roadblock. Never focus on the problem, because the problem is not the problem. Your reaction to the problem creates the true problem. It is imperative for your personal growth and goal achievement to never allow a condition to become a problem.

I have always been very open about the fact that I have dyslexia. This condition has been one of my greatest personal trials. The way my eyes see and process written words on the page has and will always be a challenge for me—a pretty daunting obstacle to overcome, as obviously I can't change the way my eyes see and process information. What I can change is my attitude toward my dyslexia, how I interpret what my eyes actually see as it translates to reading, and using any tools or resources I have at my disposal to achieve what I need to accomplish—in spite of my condition.

The backhanded gift of dyslexia is that I have developed my auditory processing and memory to a much higher level than the average person. I process and retain what I hear at a very high level to overcompensate for having a slower processing rate of what I read and see. How did this translate to my acting career, when I was starring on a daytime series, for example, and was expected to memorize up to 15 pages of new dialogue daily? I had an assistant make a recording of my lines. I would listen to them, as well as read them, several times at night before I went to bed so they would be the last thing I saw and heard before going to sleep each night. When I woke up I would go through them again one time each way and have my lines down cold when I arrived on set. Keep in mind, I still read my scripts; however, the action of listening, mentally processing and remembering what I saw and heard was a key component in my accomplishing my daily tasks to achieve my goals.

> Nothing has any power over me other than that which I give it through my conscious thoughts.

The other backhanded gift of having dyslexia is that I excel at calculating numerical data in my head and find it easy to retain the information. This proved to be a huge advantage when I worked in both the banking and mortgage industries. Calculating percentages and mortgage points comes much more easily to me than to someone who relies on writing down the information to derive the corresponding values and computations. With the right positive mental attitude, almost any obstacle can be overcome and/or turned around—and even developed into a strength.

I am sharing this to further demonstrate that obstacles don't have to stop you from achieving your goals. Dyslexia isn't a deal-breaker, just an obstacle which can be worked around for goal achievement. However, it is very important to honestly identify obstacles in your life so you can derive a plan to overcome them, work around them or at the very least just improve your attitude toward them. I may not be able to spell "sagacious," even with spell-check on the computer, but I certainly can use it in a sentence correctly faster than someone else can look it up and read the definition in the dictionary. That's not to say I am smarter or faster or better than anyone else; I'm merely providing an example of how I acknowledge an obstacle in my life and use the skills I've adapted to overcome the challenge. I refuse to allow my condition to hold me back from learning and achieving my highest personal success, in every area of my life.

Just as everyone has obstacles, everyone is blessed with innate natural gifts. What are yours? Do you know how to identify them so that you can work a backwards plan to overcome the obstacles and enhance your natural gifts?

Do not be too timid and squeamish about your actions. All life is an experiment.

I've talked at great length about the power of your own mind. Another major component to overcoming obstacles and challenges is to ensure that you don't find yourself in a pattern of self-sabotaging. Get out of your head. Fear, insecurity and uncertainty can all wreak havoc on achieving your dreams. Many people could easily achieve their wildest dreams and accomplishments. They have everything they need and more—if they would just get out of their own way!

Fear is success enemy number one. Fear is very real and absolutely does exist. It is a force powerful enough to stop countless people from accomplishing what they want to achieve. Overcoming fear requires self-confidence. Self-confidence is necessary for success. Fortunately, confidence is acquired—not innate.

Fear hates the light of truth. The moment you affirm the truth by speaking and acknowledging your fears, you take its power away and the fear will leave you. Faith comes from truth, and faith is the only thing stronger than fear.

To overcome fear you first must face it, and then take action against it. A lack of self-confidence and the presence of fear usually results from subconscious memories in your emotional memory bank. Go into that mental room and purge those old memories. Isolate them, pin them down and replace them with positive happy memories. Deposit only self-confident, success-oriented memories so when the time comes you can extract these thoughts to counter the fears when they try to present themselves.

Life's failures are stepping stones to success.

Once you have developed confidence in yourself and your abilities you will be in control of your fears. The next step is to develop these same skills for your interactions with others. Trusting yourself and building your self-confidence within yourself and in your own mind is only the first step. Practice working with people, keeping in mind that "You are important" while working on understanding the attitudes of others. Listen to what people have to say during your interactions. Do not formulate opinions until you have heard them and thought through the ideas presented. Don't merely listen to others to determine your response. Listen for understanding. Listen as a critical thinker. Listen with an open heart. Listening requires expending energy. Don't just hear someone. Process their words and decide if you want to take them in to your person or your spirit. Have the confidence in your abilities to effectively and critically listen to what others have to say. Mastering the art of effective listening is a sign of self-confidence in a successful person.

Do what your conscience tells you is the right thing to do; the right way to feel; the right way to believe. Make everything about you say: "I am confident; really, really confident'. Speak up and smile big. These rules will automatically formulate the habit of confidence in you.

- Always use big, positive, cheerful words to describe how you feel.

  (You'll start to believe it.)
- Use the same bright, cheerful words to describe other people.

  (They'll believe it and respect you with a new willingness to help.)
- Always use positive language and compliment people personally at every opportunity.
- Use only positive words to outline your plans....think it, believe it, do it...
- See what can be...not just what is...

Remember:
If you can dream it you can achieve it

When you were a child, you were free to dream countless dreams of what your future would look like, who you would become and what you could accomplish. The beauty of youth is that you don't know what you don't know and because you don't know what you can't do, you can accomplish and do anything. In your own mind, at least, all things are possible.

When kids dream about their futures, they don't know you have to go to school for more than twenty years to become a doctor or veterinarian (kindergarten through a PhD). They don't realize that becoming their favorite cartoon character's sidekick is a completely unrealistic expectation for their future, or that someone can only be a professional basketball player if they are over 6'5" tall. But then again, no one seems to have told Spud Webb that last little bit of information and look how things worked out for him in the NBA at just 5'6".

Kids don't put limits on what they imagine in their futures. Although as adults we need to be realistic in our plans to achieve our goals, we also need to reclaim that unconditional innocence of our youth. We need to allow ourselves to be free to dream.

No child ever dreams of having the statistical average of 2.5 kids, a dog, a minivan and a $200,000 mortgage for a home in the suburbs by the time they are 35. No child ever dreams of punching a time clock at a job they view as a necessary evil for supporting their family. That being said, none of the above are necessarily bad things; and none of them preclude the opportunity to attain dreams or opportunities in the future.

A true tragedy is allowing a dream to die because you're too afraid to take a chance and fail, or you're not willing to do whatever it takes to move towards achieving what makes your spirit feel alive. Let me say it again: The risk isn't the risk. The risk is not taking the risk. If we remember to shoot for the moon, when we fall short, we land in the stars. Who wouldn't want that?

Don't just show up to your regular 9-to-5 job each day, then come home to sit on the couch complaining that you'll never get what you want. Don't just sit around reminiscing about the good old days and how things used to be better. If you want to change your reality today, then you need to be doing something every day that will move you toward the fulfillment of that dream. If you aren't willing to do whatever it takes to make these dreams happen, then at least do the people around you a favor and stop complaining about where you are. Find a way to positively embrace whatever it is that you do have and whatever it is you have accomplished. Learn how to bloom where you're planted.

You may be disappointed if you fail,
but you are doomed if you don't try.

The definition of insanity is doing the same thing over and over again and expecting to get different results. So it stands to reason that if you want your life to be different, you have to do things differently. If you've decided that you're not willing to accept where you are, then complete your due diligence. In other words, do your homework. There are plenty of examples out there to emulate. Study those who have achieved something you want to achieve. Research and discover what you need to do to accomplish your own dreams... then make a plan and start doing it!

You are now at a crossroads. This is your opportunity to make the most important decision you will ever make. Forget your past. Who are you now? Who have you decided you really are now? Don't think about whom you have been, who you were. Who are you now? Who have you decided to become: Make this decision consciously. Make it carefully. Make it powerfully.

JOHN SKORY I've known Billy since we were eighteen years old... which adds up to quite a lot of years based on how old we are now! I've watched him grow up, seen him through a lot of changes, but there's one thing that has remained a constant in his life that I've always admired. Billy has the ability to set a goal, focus on making it happen, and always, absolutely achieve it. Every single time.

Back in Ohio we played football at rival high schools. After we graduated, I used to see him out at the disco clubs that were so popular back in the seventies. Throughout the years we've traveled together, I've gone to see his shows all over the U.S. and Canada, we've gone golfing all over. We've had so many good times and so many laughs. You get what you give, and he is a great friend. We talk to each other, get advice from each other, lean on each other. We have lots in common, especially our shared love for music.

The run he had on FAME was amazing... then to switch over to Days of Our Lives... there are so few people who have the ability to reinvent themselves, especially in such an unforgiving business. I completely agree with one of Billy's favorite sayings: there's no such thing as luck. Luck is when preparation meets opportunity. Billy is always prepared and always maximizes his opportunities. You create your own luck. He is a great living example of that.

He has always inspired me; to see close up his drive and how he prevailed when all odds were against him was very inspiring. He not only meets a goal, but takes it to the highest level. This is a trait I've tried hard to incorporate into my own life: to set my mind to my goals and stay the course. Unlike

Billy, however, I have been with one company for my entire career. Mine was not the common path!

I started washing trucks for the local utility company when I was seventeen years old to put myself through night school. As the years passed I rose through the ranks. Understanding what makes Billy tick and observing his climb while staying very close to him helped me immensely. Today I am president of the Cleveland Electric Illuminating Company, which has approximately 1,250 employees and is part of the giant utility FIRST ENERGY. I absolutely credit following Billy's example and practicing many of his principles throughout the years.

When we were young, whatever Billy wanted to accomplish, he did. Golden Gloves boxer. Champion dancer. Go to Hollywood... which everyone in the entire world advised against, telling him he would never make it. Of course, he proved them all wrong. Billy has the unique ability to meet whatever goal he sets for himself, no matter how far-out or unlikely it sounds. When he wakes up each morning, everything he does contributes toward meeting that goal, or else he doesn't do it. It's just that simple. To have that kind of drive and single-mindedness has brought him great success in everything he's turned his hand to.

To me success in life is about leadership, it's about people skills, it's about focus. What sets companies apart from their competitors are their people. As president of a company I think it's my job to engage people and keep them excited about coming to work every day while inspiring them to do their own personal best. When I see a kid out there in the parking lot washing trucks I know... he could be the president of the company someday. Anything can happen... Billy and I are both living proof of that!

CHAPTER THREE

Planning and Preparation

"Imagining what you want as if it already exists opens the door to letting it happen."

—Shakti Gawain

Despite what you see on *American Idol,* there are very few overnight success stories in life. When you actually take the time to examine the background of anyone who has achieved and sustained great personal success, you will no doubt realize how much hard work and dedication lay the groundwork. These people were ready, willing and able to jump on fortuitous opportunities, which eventually presented themselves at the right time, thus creating the illusion of "overnight success." Remember: true success always comes when preparation meets opportunity.

I have shared the experiences of my childhood where some seemingly huge obstacles—rheumatic fever and dyslexia—could have sidelined all of my dreams for the future. However, both turned out to be great motivators that shaped the attitude and direction that would carry me to success in multiple areas of my life. Here I would like to expound on "The rest of the story…" as the legendary late radio host Paul Harvey used to say.

As stated previously, I was a jock in my early years. My dad and uncle started training me at a very young age in the boxing ring. I had achieved athletic success boxing and on the high school football field. Twenty years after graduation, I was honored with an induction to my high school hall of fame. The success I exhibited on the field led to my receiving opportunities to play football in college. I declined these opportunities because my interests had changed. My new aspiration was to have a professional career in boxing.

As I became more successful and confident as a boxer it finally seemed to me as though I had the potential for a promising professional career. However, in 1978 I hyper-extended my right elbow and immediately ended my boxing career. All I had ever known or aspired to be revolved around my athletic abilities. Every positive label and the self-identity I prized was now shattered. I was quite abruptly at a loss for what I was going to do with my life. Still, I knew deep down that I was more than this one aspect of my life—though up to this point it had been such a prevalent, primary focus of my daily identity.

BILLY BOXING

One night during my recovery I went to a nightclub with some friends, where a woman asked me to dance. I had never been so afraid in my life. I didn't know how to dance and I still had a sling on my arm from the career-ending boxing injury. I pulled her out to the middle of the dance floor, hoping that if we were in the middle of the crowd no one would pay any attention to me or see what a bad dancer I was. But at that awkward moment, I suddenly discovered what I wanted to do for the rest of my life: Perform. And I've never looked back since. I resolved to not let a setback define my future or what I was going to achieve. I knew I didn't want to get stuck in a phase of remembering when and not achieving other dreams or moving past this chapter of my story.

When you dance, your purpose is not to get to a certain place on the floor. It's to enjoy each step along the way.

Granted, I didn't perform very well that night. Knowing that I didn't have the innate abilities as a dancer, I applied the same drive, determination and skills I applied to become successful in boxing and high school football toward becoming a good dancer. The very next day, I started seeking out classes and opportunities to enter dance competitions. I went on to compete in one hundred and eight disco competitions and won one hundred of them, and later earned the title National Dance Champion. I realized I could only go so far in disco as that genre was only going to last so long and expanded, taking classes in classical, ballet, jazz, modern and tap to broaden my skill set. It was a very humbling experience starting over at the bottom as an adult to learn new skills for the first time.

Billy Dancing

I quickly discovered that the professional dancers on the big stages like Broadway had relatively short-lived careers. Those who enjoyed sustained show business success could also sing and act, so I started to take vocal classes to develop my other skills. My goal was to become a triple threat: a performer who could sing, dance and act.

Throughout the very different paths my life took me during my early adult years, I always maintained a positive mental attitude. I was able to adapt to the adversity that came my way. I stayed open to exploring other aspects of myself—new passions and interests. I adjusted my picture of what I could accomplish and achieve and ensured that I got the proper training. I did the work required to attain each new goal and challenge I set for myself. Even though I loved music and had innate athletic abilities, I would have never achieved the success I have enjoyed as an actor, singer, dancer and musician if I had allowed the label of "jock" from high school or my accomplishments as a boxer to shape my image of myself for the rest of my life.

People often become what
they believe themselves to be.

As discussed at the beginning of this book, it's imperative to write down your dreams and goals so you can make them tangible and can more easily focus your mind on developing a plan to achieve them. We've all heard the old adage: "No one ever plans to fail. They just fail to plan." In developing your backwards plan toward achieving your goal it is critical that you create small goals and milestones to achieve along the way to the BIG goals and dreams. This strategy is two-fold. One, it keeps you feeling motivated and inspired to have a sense of accomplishment for your hard work to motivate you to continue to work hard; and two, once you reach a goal it's easier to reach the next goal because you've already achieved one and have gained some confidence. The inner power of your spirit becomes like a lion, and you develop the necessary fortitude to accomplish your dreams.

Study your failures and learn from them. Then get up and try again! Have the courage to be your own critic. Find your weaknesses and correct them. Stop blaming circumstances. Be responsible for your own life. There is a good side to almost everything, and when you find it you can defeat any sense of loss while you continue to move toward success.

> Nothing can stop the person with the right mental attitude from achieving their goal; nothing on earth can help the person with the wrong mental attitude.

I was entering dance competitions to earn money to subsidize the expense of more dance classes and ventured into modeling as well to have other streams of income. At that time a model with dance moves was in high demand. Blessedly I was booked quite often and became in high demand myself. It was clear, however, that in Cleveland, Ohio my career could only go so far. So I moved to New York City in the summer of 1979 to study dance on Broadway. Next came Hollywood, to further my aspirations for a career as an actor. I was following my passion and determined to make my dreams come true. I was working every day to master the art of reinventing myself, utilizing the skills that led to my success as an athlete to parlay into success as a performer.

I headed out west with my best friend Roberto Roman. We loaded up his old Camaro and hit the road heading west early one morning. Neither of us had ever had an acting lesson in our lives; still, we were naive enough to think we could make it in Hollywood. Roberto had one advantage over me in that he had an education and could get a regular job. I would have to get by on my skills as an entertainer; skills that still had a long way to come. In Los Angeles, I found success to be a very difficult proposition.

It had been easy to be a big fish in a small pond back home in Cleveland. Even in New York it was relatively easy to earn a living because modeling opportunities sustained me. Hollywood proved to be a completely different animal altogether. The best of the best were all in Hollywood. Everyone was beautiful. The talent level of entertainers was on an entirely different level than anything I had previously encountered. I was just another actor with huge dreams and I knew I had to change my strategy really quickly if I was going to ever have a chance to fulfill my dreams.

We had no plan, but we were young, eager, hungry and motivated. We were quite naïve about how the whole "Breaking into Hollywood" thing worked. But since we both had the "Do Whatever it Takes Mentality" at that point we tackled the challenge head on!

The thing always happens that you really believe in; and the belief in a thing makes it happen.

Plan to Work—Work the Plan

It bears repeating: Success doesn't just happen. You don't just accidentally trip and fall into it. It's not like winning the lottery (which, by the way, typically has odds of one hundred million to one on any given day). And even if by some miracle it was your day, the odds are much greater that you would spend or mismanage all of that money in a relatively short amount of time and be back at square one again anyway. Why is that? No plan.

And by the way… please don't make your plan to win the lottery. You have far greater odds at becoming President of the United States (1: 10 million), becoming a movie star (1: 1,505,000), being struck by lightning (1: 1 million) or dying in your bathtub (1: 840,000) in which case we would no longer be having this discussion, relatively speaking. So let's use those creative skills and mental acuity to develop goals to work hard and put in the necessary time and effort to make your dreams of success a reality.

People are not lazy. They simply have impotent goals—that is, goals that do not inspire them.

One suggestion for a jumping off-point is to write down where you'd like to be in every aspect of your life ten years from now. Then narrow the time span down to five years. Then three years. Then one year. Develop a backwards plan structured with short-term goals to reach the ultimate goal. Studies show that there is a direct relationship between doing work that is meaningful to us and our success at accomplishing that work. What is meaningful to each person is as unique as that particular individual. Typically it is defined as something that is complex (requires thought & skill), provides autonomy (independence/freedom) and has a direct correlation between effort and reward while allowing for creativity. If you work hard enough and assert yourself while using your mind and imagination, you can shape the world to your desires. Your only true limits are the ones you place on yourself or allow others to place on you.

Put up in a place where it's easy to see—
the cryptic admonishment T.T.T. When you feel

sometimes how slowly you climb, it's well to remember that Things Take Time.

Once you write down clearly defined goals and time frames for achieving them, you will obtain a clear fix on your desires and be better positioned to visualize the image of your goals more clearly. Set specific goals to accomplish the things you visualize for yourself. Reach the point that your brain is on autopilot to develop the habit of reaching your goals. Your thinking will automatically find and lead the way.

You will never attain the desired success or achieve your desired goals if you have the mindset that there will always be time to do it later. What if tomorrow doesn't come? What if one day you wake up and realize there's no time to do what you wanted to do or accomplish what you always wanted to accomplish. When time is gone, it's gone. We all have the same 24 hours in a day. How are you spending yours?

I find that the habits of how you spend your time correlates with how you spend your money. Are you spending it wisely? Thoughtfully? Purposefully? Or are you throwing it away like there will always be more time or more money? At some point you have to stop and look at your life and what you have or haven't accomplished. With clearly defined goals the odds are far greater that you will look back and see all of the goals you have achieved in your life as opposed to looking back at a long list of excuses for why you haven't achieved any.

God gave us two ends. One to sit on and one to think with. Success depends on which one you use. Heads you win—tails you lose.

One day soon after arriving in L.A. I went on an audition for the movie *Graduation Day*. I didn't have an appointment. No agent set things up for me. No one was expecting me. I had simply heard through the grapevine about the audition so I got myself ready and went. I was determined to read for a role that day. When I tried to charm my way past the initial gatekeeper, I found her unrelenting. It was obvious I wasn't going to get past her so I was going to have to find another way into that room.

I made my way around to the back of the building and discovered a small window open, two floors up and fairly close to a trellis. So I tucked my headshot and resume into the back of my waistband and precariously made my way up the trellis, through thorns and all, to what I was soon to discover was the women's bathroom window. Fortunately, I got in the window and out of the restroom before anyone noticed. Even more fortunately, the gatekeeper on this floor, just outside the room where casting directors were reading people, was far more amenable to my charms. It didn't matter that I wasn't on her list. I got in!

As is often the case with auditions on film projects, I never heard back on that early audition. Or so I thought. Instead I accepted a job in the dance troupe called "Dance Machine" that was the opening act for Kenny Rogers. The show was called "A Brand New Day" and was opening in Atlantic City, New Jersey at the Golden Nugget. My buddy Roberto and I were celebrating that I had gotten a job. We thought I had it made: "Welcome to Hollywood!" We were having a great time when all of a sudden some crazy guy came flying through our dumpy apartment window brandishing a large machete-like sword. We went from feeling on top of the world to just trying to stay alive in the world in a nanosecond. We subdued the would-be robber and got him out of our place. (Funnily enough, even with all of my subsequent moves, homelessness, and further adventures along the way, I actually still have that machete!)

After I arrived in Atlantic City and was working in the show, I received a call from the *Graduation Day* people—that audition I'd snuck into before I left LA. I was told I didn't get the small part I'd auditioned for but was actually cast in a larger co-starring role—the character who gets his head cut off, to be precise. That sounded great to me! I immediately packed up and quit a job that provided room, per diem and a modest weekly paycheck to head back to LA for a co-starring role in a feature film. A role I would soon find out paid $396. That was my total payment for that particular co-starring role in a feature film. I'd rolled the dice on an opportunity and busted out. Needless to say, it didn't take long for our limited funds to run out and soon enough we lost our apartment.

Roberto and I ended up parting ways as he had a corporate job opportunity and other friends to stay with for a while. I, on the other hand, suddenly found myself living on the streets. I certainly hadn't planned for this.

Adversity is your best friend on the path to success.

ROBERTO ROMAN When Billy walks into a room, he really stands out. This was true even when we were in junior high. One day Billy came over to my house; we must have been about fourteen or so. My grandmother, who lived with our family, was a very religious woman. She prayed three or four times a day and was never without her Bible, which she was constantly reading. Her faith was everything to her.

On this day Billy strolled in and she looked at him intently. She then said to me in Spanish, "Vas hacer un persona grande. Un grande artista." ("He's going to be somebody big") For her to interrupt her reading to predict, "You're going to be a star," was certainly a surprise. I was a little taken aback; the two of us were just your basic jocks, kids in Ohio. I told Billy, "Wow, my grandmother says you're going to be big. Huh.... How about that." My grandmother sensed how special he was early on. She was right. She knew.

Back in the day, that boy was just too white! He didn't have any idea how to dance! My brother and I used to beat him in all the local dance contests. It took him less than twelve months to become the best dancer I've ever seen. He put in eight hours a day, every kind of class from jazz to ballet, endless practice... he taught himself. Seriously, to this day I don't know how he did it, because I am here to attest that he had no rhythm. He was not born with any talent, trust me; he could not dance. He was a football player! But he had goals... and when he saw somebody do something and decided it was something he wanted to do? Watch out!

Eventually we both appeared on the show Dance Fever, where I beat him, which only fired him up to get even better. Less than a year later he beat me. We then decided it was time to move to LA to become stars. We drove out to Hollywood in my older brother's Camaro that ran on fumes, basically. We had some pots and pans and the shirts on our backs. And just a few bucks. We arrived in Hollywood and entered a coffee shop. We ordered and ate our breakfast, then looked across the table at each other and said, "Now what?" Fortunately Billy always made friends fast. He had met a guy on one of his previous trips to LA and called him up. This guy let us stay in his apartment one night, then the next day kicked us out. We had nowhere to go, no friends, no money, no prospects.

We found a tiny apartment complex in the middle of Hollywood and told the manager we had jobs. We used another acquaintance of Billy's as a reference, and this guy really came through for us... he told the manager of the complex, "Oh yeah, those guys are working for me." So we had our own place... well—our own room. There were plenty of growing pains along the way in Hollywood. Good times and real bad times. Without Billy I would not have made it. Flat out—no way.

Billy used to throw the change from his pockets onto the floor. When he went to Atlantic City for a month for a dancing job, I literally lived off his change. Back then you could get a hamburger at Burger King for a quarter; I used to do it every day. I survived from Billy's spare change! Whatever he did, I did too, and that's how I eventually got some acting gigs; later I got into business, earned my degree, got my first jobs.

So many kids, when they're young, have such dreams. Baseball player, doctor, actor... Billy is that one-in-a-million kid who not only has big dreams, but goes out and makes those dreams come true. He has managed to accomplish all of his goals. Everything he ever wanted to do in life, he excelled at. Sports. Acting. Singing and dancing. Achieving wealth and financial security. The business world. I don't know that many people who have managed to achieve one dream, let alone all of them! He has reinvented himself over and over in life and done well at all of them.

These days he is such an excellent coach, mentor and teacher to the kids he manages and instructs. They really look up to him; they can learn so much from somebody who relates to them so well. The way he handles life is unique. When he's auditioning, for example. The way he listens. The way he prepares. For most of my life, I watched him and learned. He has amazing street smarts, and he's not from the streets—he's from Brook Park, Ohio!

This is a man who goes after what he wants. And competitive? You have no idea. You don't want to play against Billy in a friendly basketball game. You go up against him, trust me, you are going to lose. If you're playing jacks, you are going to lose. Go up against him in an audition, you'd better bring your 'A' game. Before the audition and after the audition, he's your best friend... but you'd better believe he wants to win.

I've taken a bunch of acting classes in my life, from all kinds of teachers, and he is truly an amazing acting coach. When you're an actor, going on auditions means putting food on the table; it's your job, and it's serious. He takes an overall business approach to the whole picture of acting for a living to help his students succeed. He teaches his kids first and foremost, how to go in there and book the job. He knows they have the skills to succeed after that.

He's great to all these kids who come out to Hollywood to try to make it. I mean, let's face it, the odds are not in their favor. But the ones he takes on, he teaches. If you're a client of Billy's, he will get you in the door to take your shot at your dreams. He's fantastic with not only the kids, but their parents too.

I love Billy like a brother. And trust him implicitly. If I was ever on life support and somebody had to make that decision whether to pull the plug or not, I would want Billy to make that decision. Not my mom or family. I want Billy there in charge. Bottom line. If you're lucky enough to be a friend of Billy's, you have a friend for life. Like me!

CHAPTER FOUR

Embrace Authenticity

"Today YOU are YOU, that is truer than true.
There is no one alive that is YOUER than YOU!"

—Dr. Seuss

I had come to Hollywood with big dreams of becoming an actor. What I got was a quick and extremely harsh dose of reality. I had no apartment, no job, and virtually no money. At one point I was reduced to eating out of dumpsters to survive. This was by far the most challenging and difficult period in my life, and I do not recommend that others follow the same path when trying to achieve their dreams. The ultimate truth about those eight months is that when I changed the picture of myself in my mind, people and circumstances came together to help me get off the streets to become successful.

I clearly remember my lowest point. I had $14 to my name and was awoken in the middle of the night by someone trying to rob me. Needless to say, he was unsuccessful. I was not giving up the last bit of money I had. Right then and there I knew I needed to do something different. My circumstances needed to change.

One of the keys to success is found in inspiration or desperation. I was desperate to get off the streets. I was tired of feeling cold, hungry and desolate. I could have gone home, of course, but I stubbornly refused to give up on the dream. My family back in Ohio never knew the reality of my living situation. I didn't want them to.

> Any coward can fight a battle when he's sure of winning, but give me the man who has the pluck to fight when he's sure of losing.

At that moment my most pressing short-term goal for personal success meant just getting off the streets and having a safe place to sleep indoors at night. I remembered seeing a group of teenage boys dancing on a street corner to the beat another guy played on a simple plastic bucket. I saw all the passers-by dropping money into an old metal coffee can in appreciation of their street performance. In a short amount of time that coffee can was full of money. The light bulb went on. I thought to myself, "I can do that." So I did.

I reached out to a lady who worked at a nearby fast food restaurant who had kindly given me free leftovers on occasion. Since I was a solo act, I asked if she might have a 'boom box' I could borrow so I could play music while I danced. She came through for me, and I decided to set up a few blocks down from where I had seen those guys dancing and put on my own show. I believed I was just as talented a dancer, if not more so, and there was nothing preventing me from doing the same thing they were doing: earning cash money. In eight days I changed the circumstances of the past eight months of my life and was able to earn enough money to rent an apartment.

> Nothing ever comes to one that is worth having except as a result of hard work.

My new studio apartment certainly wasn't anything fancy but it was warm, dry and safe. My immediate short-term goal had been reached. I now had the key element in place that I needed at that time so I could focus on my next short-term goal for success. I was also able to earn enough money to buy a Suzuki 400 to get me to auditions in rain, sleet or shine. I couldn't afford anything better at the time and was, in fact, ever so grateful for everything I now did have. I could always count on that bike getting me where I needed to go. I drove it everywhere—until it fell apart, to be perfectly honest.

I re-connected with Roberto, who was sharing an apartment with several other guys and working a regular job at the time. Those eight months on the streets felt more like eight years. I went from about 170 pounds to 140 pounds in that time. Once back in a safe place I was able to take daily showers and feel good about myself again. That fed my drive and determination to be at every audition I could possibly be at every day. Changing my circumstances propelled me forward. I was determined to succeed at any cost!

Even in my darkest hours, I have always known that I was more than just the sum of my circumstances. I knew that if I maintained a positive self-image and trusted in the character traits I knew I possessed (hard-working, determined, tenacious, resourceful, dependable, kind, and honest; with both integrity and perseverance) that I could achieve any goal I set for myself. I knew that even though outwardly I had lost everything, I could still be happy. I remained determined to achieve success because I never lost sight of who I was. To quote one of my favorite mentors, Zig Ziglar, "In life, you can't always keep what you have, but you can always keep what you are."

Most people have no idea of the giant capacity we can immediately command when we focus all of our resources on mastering a single area of our lives.

I remember my first "official" audition in Hollywood as if it were yesterday. After I'd read, the casting director told my new agent that I sucked. To be more specific, he said, "This guy doesn't have what it takes to make it in this business." Needless to say, I wasn't exactly thrilled to hear that kind of feedback. I thought I had done fairly well with the scene I had prepared in advance. I'd been thrown off my game when the casting director then handed me a scene to read cold. Due to my dyslexia, I was ill-prepared for this challenge.

Hard work beats talent when talent doesn't work hard.

I knew that if I was to have any chance at succeeding - at fulfilling the dreams I had traveled across the country to accomplish—and spent eight months on the streets because I refused to give up on them—I had better start refining the skills I needed. I had to rely on the creativity, tenacity and fortitude I had utilized in the past to achieve success in other areas of my life in order to turn my dreams of making it in Hollywood a reality.

I had plenty to overcome just with my own personal look. Casting people never knew who or what I was or what ethnicity I belonged to. My ethnic background is German, Irish and Native American. I don't look white; I'm naturally darker than most. However, even with my dark complexion I don't fit the stereotypical Latin or Italian image either. I knew that every time I went in for an audition I had to immediately overcome the questions, "What is he? Where does he fit into a family?"

I had to deliver the best possible reading I could every time and be the best Billy I could be on every audition. I knew I needed to leave casting directors wanting more and wanting to fit me into the family they were casting. I also knew every time I walked into an audition that I was continuing to refine my skills and abilities to the level where I knew that I was the best Billy I could be for each performance. I may not have always been the best actor, or given the performance the casting directors were looking for, but I knew I was always the best *me.*

That's how you should be for everything you do. Be the best you that you can be. Be brave. Go for it! No one else can ever be you except you!

Trust Your Instincts

I had an opportunity to audition for one of my childhood heroes, Ivan Dixon, the only African-American actor on *Hogan's Heroes*—he played Kinch. I was very nervous. I auditioned for a WASP-y role in front of seven African-American entertainment professionals, including Topper Carew, the producer and casting director Bob Morones. I became so involved in the conversation we were having before my audition that I lost my character. When it came time to read, I sucked. There's no other word for it; I was worse than horrible. I knew I had blown it—in front of one of my heroes, no less.

This negative experience is how I developed the audition technique I now teach my students about environmental cues. This technique is one where you utilize all of your senses to fully immerse yourself in the physicality of a given scene in your mind's eye. If the scene says I am at the beach on a sunny, windy day then I must actually feel the sun warming my face, the sand between my toes and the wind in my hair; smell the fish, hear the waves. By fully immersing yourself in an environment, there is no need to act. You *become* the character because you are mentally where the scene says you are. You fully inhabit your environment.

On my way out of the audition, Ivan asked me to give it another shot—to read it the way I thought it should be read. I jumped at the opportunity to do what I knew deep down I was capable of doing. I laid it out the best I could—how I felt the character should be conveyed—trusting in myself, my creative instincts and the skills I had worked so hard to develop. When I was done, they all kindly said "Thank you." I felt much better about the audition, as they seemed to have enjoyed themselves with my second read.

Three long weeks later, after hearing nothing, I was cast as the lead guest star in the television series *Righteous Apples.* This was by far the biggest break I had had to that date. Blessedly, they enjoyed me so much in that role that they cast me in the starring role of *Clarence and the Ottaway,* a movie of the week project. The lead character in *Clarence in the Ottaway* was a basketball player who puts all of his *eggs in one basket* by focusing on only one sport. When he breaks his leg he realizes education is paramount for success in life.

Life Imitates Art. Art Imitates Life. I realized after doing this role the importance of education and that I needed to consistently be educating myself in all aspects of my art.

So it holds true:

- positivity generates positivity
- work generates work
- connections and positive impressions are remembered, generating more opportunities

Another secret of success is to do the common things uncommonly well.

Again: Live your authentic true self. No one else can be you. No one else can live your life except you. You are a one-of-a-kind original. For true success you have to tap into what you have—whatever qualities make you uniquely you. Don't be afraid to be who you are. That's where the true magic lies for achieving your dreams.

If you're an actor going on an audition, for example, there may very well be a hundred other people competing for the same one role, maybe even more. What will make you stand out to the casting directors when everyone else is delivering the same lines for the same role and has the same general look? You! That's what's unique and different: *You.* Whatever ineffable qualities you can bring to the role by being the best you that you can be. What you can bring to the role by breathing life and authentic emotion to a role makes your performance uniquely yours. What will make you stand out is the *You* that you bring to whatever role you are playing in life!

See the positive possibilities. Redirect the substantial energy of your frustration and turn it into positive, effective, unstoppable determination.

Although I had booked some parts I hadn't achieved big name recognition. I lost the lead role in *Grease 2* opposite Michelle Pfeiffer because I wasn't a big enough "name" and didn't have enough credits. In retrospect, clearly everything happens for a reason and in its own time. By staying true to who I was and keeping clear on my goals, while having the tenacity to persevere with a positive mental attitude in spite of the many obvious adversities facing me, I was able to start achieving success and accomplishing my goals. Getting off the streets had set in motion a series of events that eventually led to the audition that would forever change my life.

Ironically, one year after the humbling professional assessment of my acting abilities, I would walk into the first audition for the life-changing role of Christopher Donlon on the groundbreaking television series *Fame,* only to see the casting director who had stated I sucked in my very first audition. He had not laid eyes on me since our first inauspicious encounter, and my initial gut feeling was that I didn't stand a chance with this guy. I was already so stressed and my stomach so upset that I had cold sores—not the best look at an audition, when you're trying to put your best face forward.

At this early initial stage I knew they were looking to fill the traditional All-American look—"blonde hair/blue eyes." I was also well aware that I didn't fit that look. What I lacked in looks I had to ensure that I made up for in tenacity, fortitude and determination. I knew I had to give this audition process everything I had. I knew how hard I had worked the previous year to train myself in techniques for cold readings and how to quickly memorize scripts. I also knew I had to immediately push past my negative thinking. I had to trust in the hard work and diligent training I had worked on every day. To my shock and amazement, the feedback this time from the casting director was that I was wonderful.

More than 40,000 young men had auditioned across the nation for the one new open role on the hit television series *Fame.* Over the course of the next four months I had eleven callbacks, which ultimately led to a final audition. I knew that this was my last shot in front of the casting directors and executive decision-makers, so I had to give it everything I had in me—lay it all out on the table, so to speak, for this one last shot at this one particular role.

After the endless ongoing auditions and cast match-ups, we were down to the final four guys and four women who were vying for the two open roles (one male and one female) on the series. I was scheduled to go in first. For this type of audition situation, that was the ideal position to be in. My scene partner had just wrapped a major movie project and wasn't sure if she was even interested in doing a television series, so she had hardly prepared and hadn't memorized all of her lines. I knew I would be in trouble if I went in first.

BILLY—UP CLOSE AND PERSONAL MAGAZINE INTERVIEW DURING FAME DAYS

I asked the casting director if I could switch to last place. He strongly discouraged this idea, assuring me that this was my audition to lose. He was really rooting for me to book the job, so he did everything in his power to persuade me to not make the switch. Basically, he thought I was nuts and hurting my chances. I respectfully stated that I understood what he was saying but was sure this move would be best for me. I didn't want to throw my scene partner under the bus, but I also knew I had to be prepared for what I intuitively felt would happen in the audition scene.

The casting director finally relented, and I used the extra time to read with my scene partner. This way I could actually memorize her lines in addition to my own. When it was our turn to read she messed up, as I had known she would. Since I was prepared for this eventuality I prompted her with a cue, impressing everyone in the room. And sure enough, I booked the job of a lifetime and it changed my life substantially, in the most positive way. A great takeaway lesson from this process: patience. If I had gotten the role in *Grease 2,* I might not have ever auditioned for *Fame* or subsequently landed the role on a #1 show that ultimately changed my life forever. Through booking this one role, I became one of the biggest teen idols of the 80's.

FAME'S PHOTO SHOOTS

If I hadn't 1) had the positive mental attitude and firm belief that I was more than my circumstances; 2) gotten off the streets by being open to an unconventional way of earning money (legally, ethically and morally) to change my circumstances; and 3) known in the very core of my being that I was good enough to accomplish my goals and dreams, I could not have achieved a new reality. Within the span of about a year and a half, I went from eating out of dumpsters to flying on a private jet around the world.

The risk is not the risk. The risk is not taking the risk.

"I've never had an original thought."
—Dr. Lehman Strauss

I recently heard the above quote by Dr. Lehman Strauss, a notable theologian. His words really shocked me: "I've never had an original thought." That's quite a surprising statement to someone who has spent half his adult career earning a living in a profession where creativity, individuality and originality are paramount. However, the more I thought about it, the more the wisdom behind this concept resonated with me as I looked back on the successes of my life.

Dr. Strauss believed that every thought he had ever had, or would have in the future, was a thought someone else in the history of the world had already had as well. The only difference was what he did, or didn't do, with those thoughts.

It has been said that each of us are the sum total of all of the experiences in our lives. If you humbly take a step back for a moment to examine the sum total of your words, deeds, thoughts and actions, it's easy to see the wisdom in those words.

In my case, I know that I have gleaned as much information as possible from those whom I deem highly successful in business, their personal lives or both. Over the years I have voraciously consumed the teachings of as many of the best motivational, professional and inspirational speakers, writers and personal mentors that I could. What I have taken to heart from these many experiences is that the core principles of these various teachings are universally true. My own successes have not been a matter of reinventing the wheel, merely reiterating and refining the same universal concepts that have led others to their successes. What matters is how I take ownership of the information and apply it to my daily life. It is in this way that new knowledge, combined with my own wisdom, experiences and observations, continues to add to and shape the universal truths in my life.

Ironically, just as I began the journey of writing this book, the Super Bowl aired a commercial that perfectly exemplifies this exact concept. Several scenes play out showing conversations between a husband and wife, in different parts of the world, with the man in each scenario claiming that he has "the best idea in the world… no one else has ever thought of this before…" Did you see the commercial? What happened next? You can probably guess the answer whether you saw the commercial or not: many others had had the same *'brilliant'* idea, yet only one acted on it and capitalized on his thought with his subsequent actions.

Makes you stop and think for a moment, doesn't it? What brilliant ideas or thoughts have you had that you haven't acted on? What brilliant ideas or thoughts do you have now that you want to act on? More to the point, what is your plan for action?

The truth is there's nothing you can't accomplish if you set your mind to accomplish a goal or task. You need to clearly define what you want to achieve and create a backwards plan to get there. Stay open and flexible to take a different route or be willing to reinvent yourself along the way. The path to success is never an easy, uncomplicated straight line. What's the challenge in that? It's a journey with hills and valleys and roadblocks. The real question is: Are you going to happen to your life or let life happen to you?

BILLY, WHEN HE STARRED AS EMILIO RAMIEREZ
ON *DAYS OF OUR LIVES*

CHAPTER FIVE

Ready for Reinvention

"It's never too late to be who you might have been."
—George Elliot

As blessed as I was for the opportunity of playing a lead role in the biggest series in the world, the reality is that the role of Christopher Donlon in *Fame* typecast me. I was now known worldwide as the kid from *Fame*. I was a teen idol. I was known for having the number one bestselling poster when I posed in a towel just out of a shower. That old saying is true: Be careful what you wish for; you might actually get it. I had wished for a successful acting role in Hollywood and I got it. What I failed to realize was how easy it was to get painted into a box and be seen forevermore for only one role, not as an actor who could play all kinds of characters.

> If you don't set a baseline standard for what you'll accept in life, you'll find it's easy to slip into behaviors and attitudes or a quality of life that's far below what you deserve.

BILLY ON *DAYS OF OUR LIVES*
AS EMILIO RAMIREZ

When *Fame* ended I had to rely on my skills for reinventing myself and having the tenacity and fortitude to persevere if I was ever going to work in Hollywood again. I did some small roles and appeared in television shows like *Baby Talk* with Scott Baio and *Married with Children* playing the role of Zoro—in an attempt to change the image everyone had of me as a "Teen Idol." I knew I had to change my image from that of a boy to a man.

Once again, perseverance paid off. I landed the role of Emilio Ramirez on the daytime series *Days of our Lives*—a man's role. This brought on a whole new set of challenges to overcome. Being dyslexic, it was an arduous task to memorize any lines. Being on a daytime series, that task increased exponentially. I was now responsible for approximately 15 pages of new dialogue daily. I had to develop new skills and ways to achieve my daily goals for my new job.

Now that I was free from the typecast box of being merely a teen idol or the kid from *Fame,* I was blessed to work solid on numerous projects and entertainment jobs for the next decade—right up until I was diagnosed with the Big C: Cancer.

A strong positive mental attitude will create more miracles than any wonder drug.

BILLY JUST BEFORE CANCER DIAGNOSIS

Approximately fifteen years ago I was starring in a theatrical production in Akron, Ohio. One of the dancers spotted a small something she thought looked odd on my face. There was a questionable-looking spot on the edge of my lip and another one on the bridge of my nose near my eye. Over the course of the next few weeks the spots grew bigger, so I went to the doctor and was told I had to have surgery immediately. I had skin cancer on my face in two places. And I had a tumor on my lower back. To complicate things further, during my post-operative recovery I acquired a staph infection that almost ended my life.

At the time, I was toying with the idea of entering the political arena back home in Cleveland, Ohio. The Big C can put all of your plans, thoughts, ideas and dreams for the future on hold. Treatment was necessarily swift and immediate. After that I certainly had a completely different perspective on life. Time, family, friends, and life in general all seemed to speed up. I had an overwhelming sense of urgency to accomplish everything I could and every dream I had yet to achieve. I think anyone facing cancer would agree that what is truly important in life comes into much sharper, clearer focus, providing some immediate clarity about priorities.

Obviously, the Big C didn't win because I'm still here; and still reinventing myself every day. After that health crisis I chose to walk away from my career in the entertainment industry. I chose to stop my forward momentum on the particular path I was on. I wanted to set new goals, re-invent myself and accomplish other dreams that I had for myself in this lifetime.

It's not because things are difficult that
we do not dare. It is because we do not dare
that they are difficult.

During my 20+ years earning a living as a performer I had always been involved in investment real estate on various different levels. Since one of these ventures had been as an owner of a mortgage brokerage company, now dissolved, I thought I would try my hand in the corporate environment of investment banking. I started in the mortgage division of World Savings Bank in Las Vegas, Nevada, and worked my way up the ladder to the position of Director of Business Development.

When I started my new job I wasn't accepted at all. I was entering an industry where I was now competing against college graduates. I had to cut my hair, take out my earrings and conform to the typical conservative dress code of a successful corporate American businessman. I did the best I could at all times and received numerous promotions over the years that benefited me financially. Furthermore, the work provided the perfect opportunity for me to learn from the inside how corporate America really functions. I gained invaluable insight into an industry I had never experienced on that level previously.

Early in my entertainment career, when I started earning substantial money, I studied financially successful people to discover the commonalities to their success. I discovered that the only way to become truly financially successful is by finding a way to first, make your money make money for you; and second, to earn money while you sleep. I did my research and that answer for me was real estate. My first purchase was an apartment building. When I started to make money at real estate I never quit my day job, as a performer or later in banking. I never stopped doing what I was doing on a normal daily basis to earn a living. Real estate was an investment, not my primary job. I built up that first apartment building and rolled it into other properties, which led in turn to more developments and properties. I continued working my day job the entire time, knowing I could never count on real estate as my primary source of income since the market is typically so volatile. With this mindset, when the crash of 2009 occurred it wasn't as financially devastating for me as it had been for others I knew who depended on real estate as their primary source of income.

So many people in America live paycheck to paycheck. So many Americans are just a few paychecks away from being homeless as they don't have the savings or a financial cushion to sustain themselves through lean times. After the crash of 2009, even many of those who did have a financial cushion exhausted their reserves while seeking ways to reinvent themselves and regain stability.

Since the harsh economic realities hit home in 2009, many people find it difficult to feel secure anymore. They are always worried that they will lose their job, lose the money they have tried to regain, lose their spouse, lose their health, etc. The only true security in life comes from knowing that every single day you are improving yourself in some way; that you are increasing the caliber of who you are and that you are valuable to your company, your friends and your family.

Take control of your emotions and
begin to consciously and deliberately reshape
your daily experience of life.

BILLY AT AGE 55—
RECLAIMING HIS FITNESS AND HEALTH

As the years passed I continued to rise through the ranks and amass some substantial wealth through my real estate investments. Then once again I had a health crisis. I was misdiagnosed as having had a stroke. After many months of doctors, tests, medicines and a borderline deep depression caused by the frustration of not finding any answers, it was finally determined that I hadn't suffered a stroke after all. I had three displaced disks in my neck due to injuries I had sustained decades prior as a boxer, which caused paralysis and droopiness in my face, arm and upper chest on my left side. To be honest, it was a long, horrible, stressful journey to get the answers I was seeking for my deteriorating health and physical condition. I had never experienced anything so scary. At one point during the testing/discovery phase of this journey I was suspected of having a brain tumor. In one more medical misstep I was prescribed a pain medication that left me feeling suicidal. The whole thing was just nuts because I have always been so in tune with knowing my body and had lost control of it during this process.

Over the course of this health crisis I gained sixty pounds, had no energy and generally felt incredibly miserable most days. Once I finally received a proper diagnosis and a course of treatment was set that helped me get back on track, I knew I had to go all the way to re-claiming my physique. I no longer liked who I saw reflected back at me in photographs. Now that I was armed with the information and answers I needed, I was going to reclaim my body to be the best that I could possibly be—again.

Now that I was once again in-tune with the small, still voice inside of me, I knew that it was once again time for a major change. Even though I had achieved great success in the world of corporate banking I knew that I now needed to do something different. I knew that I would find true joy again by tapping back into my creative side and following a career path that afforded me an opportunity to be in touch with creativity and imagination and people who shared similar dreams and aspirations.

Do not go where the path may lead; go instead where there is no path and leave a trail.

When the economic crash of 2009 occurred, it didn't bankrupt me like it did so many others because I had never quit my 'day job.' I never made real estate my sole source of income or my main career. When Wachovia offered a buy-out program I gladly took it and ran. It was the perfect opportunity to shift primary careers while waiting for the real estate markets to recover.

Interestingly enough, the experience and ideas I initially brought to the table hadn't originally been embraced, but by the time I decided to move on, nearly three years later, the upper echelon of the bank that I was working for were busily implementing many of my ideas based on my experience from previously owning a successful mortgage company. These strategies had previously not been accepted as the norm in their corporate business models. Times had changed, and I was changing with them.

We cannot direct the wind,
but we can adjust the sails.

BILLY AND SCOTT BAIO—*CONFESSIONS OF A TEEN IDOL*

After the buyout from the banking business, my friends Scott Baio and Jason Hervey asked me if I wanted to participate in a new reality series they were producing called *Confessions of a Teen Idol.* It seemed that life was coming full circle. The image I'd worked so hard to shake as a performer was one that I was now being paid to highlight and explore.

I knew that show business was an unforgiving industry that didn't give many second chances, so I had to take every opportunity I could during this second go-round. It was my first introduction to the genre of reality television.

I quickly learned that the reality of reality TV is that you have no control over how they edit the footage they have captured or how they are going to portray your 'character' through the editing process. Producers and story editors can easily splice a comment or a look on your face with an image or reaction shot of someone else to make it look like your look or comment was directed to a particular person, one who might not have been in any way involved in that situation or even in a completely different day or week of filming.

In scripted television you know what the action is going to be when you show up for work. You know what the boundaries are going to be in advance. You know what to expect. With reality, producers like to create friction and capture drama so they can make what they feel is more compelling television for the viewing audience. You never know what's going to happen on a daily basis and you always have to stay on your guard.

I seized the opportunity and had a great time doing it. At one point on the show they pitted us against each other for a lucrative hair commercial (Aussie hair products). The character description was, "25-year-old with a great head of hair with a great body." This would have been perfect for me—twenty-five years ago! Now I was competing against some of the former teen idols who were still in their 20's and 30's. I got as creative as I could and just went for it because I knew I wasn't what they were looking for. What I lacked in youth and great hair, I made up for in tenacity and fortitude to bring the best Billy I could to the audition. I wore zebra striped spandex pants and went for it on top of a Jaguar. I did the splits holding a guitar. Laid it out! Went for it! Once again, reinvention and creativity worked. I got the job and shot the commercial for Aussie Hair Products. If you believe you *can* achieve—and that day—it went my way!

The timing was perfect because I capitalized on the timing of the TV show to further develop and build up my emerging new brand as a coach and (eventually) personal manager. Once again, I was back to my first and truest passion—entertainment.

As human beings, our greatness lies not
so much in being able to remake the world,
as in being able to remake ourselves.

BRIAN "B.J." BOSTIC After I graduated from college, I moved out to Los Angeles to pursue a job in the entertainment business. I gave myself six months to make it. After four months I hadn't gotten very far; I was working at a wine brokerage making cold calls, which was not at all what I wanted to do. Money was running low. I was at a crossroads. Through family connections a meeting was arranged with Billy. I went out to his house and handed him my resume. He basically tossed it aside and said, "You're not going to make it in the entertainment business with this background... where's your film degree, for one thing?" I left our meeting quite deflated.

The next morning at 5am Billy called me. "Bring a pen and pad of paper and meet me at Jerry's Deli for an appointment." That was the start of our relationship. Because of my interest in entertainment, Billy arranged some production assistant jobs for me... enough for me to see that really wasn't what I wanted to do with my life after all. As I got to know Billy better I heard quite a lot of his stories. I thought, This guy really is quite an actor – telling tales. As time passed, I realized that everything he said was actually true. All these incredible life experiences had really happened. You'd think one person couldn't possibly have done all these things. But he truly had; it was pretty amazing.

One day Billy said, "I've got an unbelievable opportunity. I've been offered a great position within a large institution, World Savings Bank in Las Vegas. They want me to come in and basically transform this department. I'm going to try to get them to find a place for you there too." That's the thing about Billy... he knows so many people from all over, every kind of industry, that all kinds of opportunities present themselves to him.

Billy became the area sales manager for the mortgage home loans division. He managed to arrange a great job for me, even though I had zero experience. My position was basically shadowing him, which I did for the next two years. Billy certainly did things differently than the other banking executives. He was in charge of staffing – finding the people who were going to do the actual sales. He hired an amazing array of men and women from every kind of background to work in the office. He probably had a dozen employees each with a unique cultural background for servicing the very diverse international community of Las Vegas.All these personalities made for quite an interesting office... certainly the bank had never seen one like it before!

Typically, mortgage people would build a relationship with realtors and bring them to their office to make their pitch. Billy took a different approach... he went after the real estate offices. He asked realty companies if we could place one of our staffers in their office at a regular desk. This person would sit there full-time every day and be available for any and all mortgage or loan questions. That was a brilliant move; some of these offices employed a hundred or more realtors, and we had someone right there in house at each of them.

He did a great job with lots of creative flair until the real estate crash hit, devastating real estate and mortgage brokers nationwide. Still, we fared better than most. We were both given severance packages from the bank, and I used mine to buy a rental property in Las Vegas based on Billy's advice. That's been a successful investment for me, one I still own, and I have Billy to thank.

At that point we parted ways for awhile and I took a position at a wealth management company. Eventually I returned to work with Billy for another year. I liked what we were doing, but I wasn't passionate about it. And this is probably the most valuable lesson among many I learned from Billy Hufsey. He sat me down one day and got very real and direct with me, which I appreciated. He encouraged me to pursue a job that would truly excite me. The wide array of experiences I had working with him were a huge plus in helping me land my dream job. Today I work for a large Fortune 500 company in sales management.

Meeting Billy at that crucial moment changed everything. I have him to thank for many invaluable lessons in business and in life.

CHAPTER SIX

Persevere

"The difference between perseverance and obstinacy is that one comes from a strong will, and the other from a strong won't."

—Henry Ward Beecher

I credit my mother with teaching me that even when you think you have exhausted every possibility when trying to achieve a goal, you can always find the strength to give it one more try. That one more shot just might be the breakthrough that leads to success. This attitude led to my lifelong philosophy that can be summed up by what I always tell my students now: *"Persistence Breaks Resistance."*

As I have recounted, throughout my youth I heard repeatedly how I couldn't do certain things. All this did was fuel my determination to ensure that I *could* do it, whatever the '*it*' was I supposedly couldn't do! When I was told I was too small for sports like football, I worked on my body to build strength. When I was told there wasn't extra money in the family budget for the activities I was interested in, I created my own income so I could take the class I wanted or buy the bike I had to have. I knew I was responsible for my own destiny, and the only limitations I truly faced were those I placed on myself. Not limitations others wanted to place on me!

Let fear be a counselor, not a jailor.

As an aspiring performer, I recall being told more than once I couldn't play the guitar, the drums, the piano, the saxophone, the trumpet… you get the picture. I was told that my singing skills and overall musical abilities were less than mediocre. My performance skills were deemed so-so. I took every bit of all that negative criticism and channeled it into a steadfast determination to be the best performer I could be in each and every area. Subsequently, in later years when I toured the world for *Fame,* I performed onstage in front of hundreds of thousands of concertgoers who appreciated my talents. The criticisms of the few should never determine the limitations on what you know you can achieve. I removed the labels others put on me and replaced them with tenacity, fortitude and most importantly, perseverance.

> It's not what's happening to you now, or what has happened in your past that determines who you become. Rather, it's your decisions about what to focus on, what things mean to you, and what you're going to do about them that will determine your ultimate destiny.

Remember: success comes when preparation meets opportunity. What you do today—determines who you are tomorrow. As an acting and singing coach I find myself repeating that phrase nearly every day of every single week. Why? Because I am reminded of how appropriate that phrase is every single day! This mantra bears repeating. Let it sink into your mind and into your spirit. Take ownership of it. Always strive to learn. Continually work toward your goals. Keep the ship moving forward, even when setbacks and/or obstacles occur. Overnight success is a fluke; hard work and preparation will always pay off eventually if you keep working toward your goals.

Learning and growing as a person are never-ending processes. The single greatest challenge we face in life is discovering who we are; the second greatest is being happy with what we have discovered. The good news is that you have an opportunity to learn something new and grow every day. It doesn't matter what you are learning: something about yourself personally, more about the people in your life, your community, your everyday surroundings or a faraway vacation; anywhere and everywhere, the possibilities for learning something new every day are endless.

Remember, it takes at least 21 days to make a new behavior become a habit. Even then, it is all too easy to fall back into the old patterns in our lives when we get busy simply getting through day-to day-life. Aristotle said it best: "We are what we repeatedly do. Excellence then is not an act but a habit."

The Magic of 10,000

As I hope I have firmly established by now, in spite of my dyslexia I have always had a voracious appetite to learn and acquire information through various sources. I continually strive to better myself and improve the lives of those close to me through sharing knowledge. My two greatest areas of interest are the motivational/self-improvement/business world and the field of medicine. I am sure the former is obvious as they impact my world both personally and professionally, but the latter may come as a surprise. Medical terms and medicines are based on Latin and therefore the words look the way they sound. Given my dyslexia, they are much easier to read. The medical field has always been fascinating to me. My constant researching helps me to better understand my own medical challenges.

The first concept of what I think of as the "Magic of 10,000" is presented by the author Malcolm Gladwell in the book *Outliers, The Story of Success,* a book that appeals to my first area of greatest interest. Throughout the book, Malcolm shares his research findings on the different elements that come into play in the lives of highly successful people. He dedicates an entire chapter to conveying that it takes approximately 10,000 hours to master a certain art or skill, which in turn leads to success at whatever your *thing* is in life. He details specific examples of some notably successful people such as Bill Gates, Bill Joy, Mozart and the Beatles, to name a few. He does point out that not everyone who dedicates this level of time and commitment will necessarily become successful; however, one cannot become successful without it. Here's an excerpt that particularly resonated with me from this section of his book:

> "The emerging picture from such studies is that ten thousand hours of practice is required to achieve the level of mastery associated with being a world-class expert—in anything," writes the neurologist Daniel Levitin. "In study after study, of composers, basketball players, fiction writers, ice skaters, concert pianists, chess players, master criminals, and what

have you, this number comes up again and again. It seems that it takes the brain this long to assimilate all that it needs to know to achieve true mastery."[1]

When I look back at the successes in my own life I can honestly say that I probably invested at least that many hours in the mastery of many different skills. I spent countless hours in the boxing ring developing the skills required to become a Golden Gloves boxer. I spent every day of every week for years in numerous dance classes, acquiring mastery of those skills in a career path that I came to (relatively) late in life. I knew I had to voraciously learn and practice to catch up to where others my age, dancing since childhood, were in order to be competitive. I spent, and still spend, countless hours working on the development of my musical and vocal skills, training my ear to hear subtleties in sound most don't even notice. I spent, and still spend, countless hours studying the real estate market, housing trends and how I can best capitalize on trends to maximize a return on my investments.

Create a vision and never let the environment, other people's beliefs, or the limits of what has been done in the past shape your decisions.

My life has been all about persistence and pursuing something I am truly passionate about in every different field

[1] "Outliers, The Story of Success," Malcolm Gladwell, 2008, Little Brown and Company

I try my hand at. If you don't have passion for something, you won't invest that level of time and commitment to learning and developing a skill or talent. Again, I don't share my accomplishments to brag about myself, but merely to show you that with enough persistence, if you truly want something, you can achieve it. You can accomplish your dreams and your goals, whatever they may be, if you are willing to invest the required level of time and repetition required for mastery.

This research reiterates that there are no overnight successes. Sure, there are those we have seen throughout the years who acquire their "fifteen minutes of fame," but is that really true mastery of something for sustainable long-term success? That only comes with the ability to capitalize on that "fifteen minutes" and maneuver it into something that will garner long-term results. You never want to become the homeless professor who believed he was only capable of one thing, and if he couldn't do that one thing he couldn't, and wouldn't do anything at all.

The next time the concept of 10,000 came up was when I heard about research presented by Dr. Karyn Purvis, the Director of the Institute of Child Development at Texas Christian University in Fort Worth, Texas. This touched on the second area of great interest to me, medical research. In a nutshell, Dr. Purvis basically conveyed that it takes 10,000 times of repeatedly doing something to develop new pathways in the brain. For example, with a newborn baby you establish trust and convey a message of being reliable to your child when they cry and you pick them up. With babies, most of us probably know that you quickly achieve 10,000 times of repeating this particular action, which in turn establishes a bond of trust. Babies learn that if they cry, you will be there to pick them up.

The concepts that Dr. Purvis presented contradicts earlier medical research I have read, which indicated that every part of the brain has developed by the age of three, and areas of the brain not stimulated prior to this time could never be developed.

In both of these very different examples, the magic number is 10,000. It takes that many hours of practice or that many repetitions of a certain action to achieve mastery of something or light up new connections in your brain. For me, this was a light bulb realization—because both instances clearly demonstrate to me that if you truly want something you can achieve it. It is within your power to dedicate that many hours to the mastery of an art or skill. You can choose to dedicate repeating an action 10,000 times to develop a skill or wire new pathways in your brain. It's never too late to get started. It's never too late to learn something new. It's never too late to decide to pursue a dream or goal. You just have to have the passion and desire to go for it!

Not to dream boldly may turn out to be simply irresponsible.

JOHN DAQUINO I've known Billy for probably 35 years now... since he was the Disco King of Cleveland, Ohio. Back in the day Billy was like Tony Manero in Saturday Night Fever. When he walked in, all the heads turned... and could he ever take over a dance floor. At the time I met him Billy was talking about coming out to LA to become an actor... and he certainly succeeded beyond anyone's wildest expectations.

One of Billy's best qualities is his loyalty. He got very famous for a number of years in the late eighties – starring on Fame, working on Days of our Lives... and we still hung out all the time. He continued to call, stay in touch, invite me to whatever party or event he had going. I lived in Los Angeles too, so I was along for his whole Hollywood ride, and it was a blast! "Hey, I've got a huge suite in Palm Springs next weekend... let's go!" Or "The Academy Awards parties are all coming up, come with me!" He always remembered his buddies from the old days and included them. From that day to this.

Hanging out with him inspired me in many ways. Billy has always been incredibly physically fit and a great athlete. His commitment to eating well and staying in shape impressed me. I was hanging out with him, and a bunch of other people who looked like him and shared those values. Birds of a feather. He inspired me to go to the gym every day for a couple of hours and adopt a healthy diet. I have kept up my weight lifting regime for at least twenty years now, and it has done me a world of good to take care of my body and mind in this way.

If there is one word I would use to describe my friend, it's relentless. I remember him practicing dance moves endlessly back in Ohio. For hours and hours, day after day, week after week, until he got it. Billy never gives up once he has a goal. He will master it -- then it's on to the next thing. There are very few things he doesn't do well, and he always plays to win. You play a friendly game of Ping Pong with Billy, he'll cream you. Shoot a friendly game of pool in a bar, he will kill you. Bowling, shooting a pickup game of basketball... you name it, he's good at it and he will beat you at it. Period.

He is also a master of reinvention. These days he's reinvented himself once again – this time as a manager and coach. One again he's managed to succeed, in such an unforgiving business. I will never forget how he called me up a few years ago and said, I'm having a holiday party at my house, I want you to come... Of course I went. I pulled up to his house, walked inside and almost lost it. There were four hundred kids in there running around! I'm not even exaggerating, there had to be four hundred of them, ranging in age from six to eighteen, plus their parents! I was almost speechless. I found the host and asked, "What the hell is going on here Billy?"

"Dude, I've got an acting studio, I'm helping these kids become singers, and dancers, and actors... wait till you see, they're great..."

The man's home was literally overrun with all these kids in every room reciting monologues, dancing, singing... It was a madhouse! I had a fun time at this party, and Billy was right, some of those kids were amazingly talented, but I was completely surprised by this turn of events. It was a little different from his eighties parties, let me put it that way!

Then, for the next few years, Billy started hanging out with this one particular kid. Everywhere we went he was accompanied by this random fourteen-year-old boy. Everything we did, there'd he'd be. They were glued at the hip. "This kid's gonna be a star," he'd tell me. "Sing something for Johnny!" And this kid would, and he was good, but I didn't take Billy's pronouncements too seriously. I was always polite, and would say something encouraging like, "You sound great." I'm an optimist, and I wish everyone the best, but I didn't think much more than this was just Billy's little sidekick.

Then one holiday weekend I was just hanging out on my couch, watching the Macy's Thanksgiving Day Parade, and I did a double take. "Is that... James up there on the float?" Sure enough, there was the kid... and after that, I couldn't turn around without seeing him. On floats, on huge billboards all over Sunset Boulevard... there he was, James Maslow... he had become a star! The kid has done quite well for himself. Billy was in his corner and look what happened. It was no accident. Relentless, remember?

CHAPTER SEVEN

Nurture Your Spirit

"You can have everything in life you want, if you will just help enough other people get what they want."

—Zig Ziglar

Earlier in this book I touched on some of the character traits that led to my success in overcoming adversity, obstacles and setbacks. The one constant in my life has always been and will always be ME. The one thing that is always within my power to control and change at any time is my character, which in turn affects my attitude, my ability to set goals and achieve them and the entire direction for the course I want my life to go in.

Numerous studies have outlined the commonalities and character traits of highly successful people. Regardless of their beginnings in life and the obstacles or adversities these people faced, the same basic principles and character traits existed within them all. Before we delve further into the actual character traits associated with highly successful people, let's take a closer look at what constitutes character, according to dictionary.com:

- The aggregate of features and traits that form the individual nature of some person or thing.
- One such feature or trait; characteristic.
- Moral or ethical quality: *A man of fine, honorable character*
- Qualities of honesty, courage, or the like; integrity: *It takes character to face up to a bully.*
- Reputation: *A stain on one's character.*

It is important to keep in mind that character is not what we have or own; it is not what people think of us; it is not a list of our accomplishments or our successes. Character is who we are. One of the best-known quotes about character reminds us that, "Character is what you do when no one is looking."

You don't need to be better than anyone else,
you just need to be better than you used to be.

Over a period of time, a person's character will always work its way to the surface and become apparent to everyone around them. Character isn't something you can fake or buy; it has to be earned one choice at a time. Character can be developed, enhanced and improved upon with concerted effort and daily practice, and by remaining cognizant of our choices, decisions and thoughts on a daily basis. Evidence of a person's character will manifest itself in someone's personal and professional life, as well as in their health, relationships, finances and spiritual life. Conversely, underdeveloped character qualities can cause major negative ramifications in every aspect of our lives.

> When the choice is to be right or to be kind,
> always make the choice that brings peace.

Now that we have examined what character is and isn't, and know that it can be developed in our own lives, let's examine the character traits of highly successful people so we can evaluate how to develop them for our own personal success.

Some of the first traits that immediately come to mind are:

Tenacity
Fortitude
Non-complacent

Perseverance

Honesty

Integrity

Respect

Trustworthiness

Fairness

Forgiveness

Self-motivated

Driven… not selfish—there's a fine line between the two

Having a servant's heart—meaning to choose to be of service within your family and community.

These general principles are universal and transcend cultures, genders, and socioeconomic levels.

It's also imperative to keep in mind that throughout our lives you may very well have to deal with people who do not possess these traits or are simply not invested in the importance of developing positive, success-driven character traits for themselves. You must remain cognizant of your own words, deeds, thoughts and actions to not allow others to bring you down. This is not to say that you are better than someone else if you have a positive character and theirs seems somewhat lacking; this is just to say that you should not only love people right where they're at, but you should also try to be a positive influence on other's character. Remember: positivity begets positivity. If it becomes obvious that you are dealing with a person who is non-responsive to the positivity and character of how you choose to live, it may become necessary to walk away.

Be kind whenever possible. It is always possible.

When you give of your time and talents it's important to remember that you are giving of yourself freely because you choose to give of yourself—not for anything you will personally gain. There will be times in your life that the gift of sharing your time and talents will not be received or appreciated in the same space and spirit from which it was offered. Even if you pour your time and talents into a person or project with all of your heart, there is always the possibility that your efforts will not be appreciated or respected.

Remember that you are only in control of yourself. This is a very freeing realization: You can only alter and change your own perceptions, your own character, your own words, deeds, thoughts and actions. Be the person to others that you want people to be toward you. You will be surprised to find that others will intuitively start to mirror your actions and behaviors. Be the positive force you'd like to see in your world. Many others will follow your lead. If they don't change, then accept their attitude and let it go. Or just simply let them go from your life.

In letting go, a key for success with this is in possessing the character trait of forgiveness. If you aren't able to forgive someone, holding on to that anger and negativity will eventually grow like a disease within you and destroy your light, your happiness and your personal achievements. Forgiving someone who has wronged you isn't about the person you are forgiving. Forgiveness is about freeing yourself. Forgiveness is about loving yourself enough to allow you to move past the negative experience requiring the act of forgiveness.

Treat everyone with politeness, even those who are rude to you—not because they are nice, but because you are.

And trust me—I know how hard this can be. I do not deal well with betrayal or deception from those in either my personal or professional life. I've experienced a million-dollar business betrayal. That experience was a pretty definitive kick in the gut kind of betrayal. But what I know to be true is that living in the space of the anger, frustration and darkness of that betrayal is not the way I want to live my life. I had to free myself from that darkness to free myself to move past it and on to achieve other success. Just as in other obstacles I have overcome to achieve success in multiple areas of my life, I chose to not stay in that negative space. I chose to move past it. And I chose to forgive and let it go. I trusted those on my team to deal with the legalities involved. And I trust in a higher power that enables me to believe that I am to grow and learn from every experience I encounter to become a better version of myself and continue on the path to achieve success in my life.

We're all here to complete our own journey. Some people come into our lives for a short period of time and others for a lifetime. Some grow up and grow together. Others grow up and grow apart. Some experiences are positive and we grow from them. And others can be negative and we can chose to grow from them as well. Everyone's journey and path is different and unique to their own belief that they are pursuing their dreams, ambitions and personal success story. No one ever truly knows the dreams in your heart other than you. No one can live your life except you. The choice to live it purposefully or to merely live if by default is yours and yours alone.

Character is who you are
when no one is watching.

In previous chapters I have touched on the concept of owning my own businesses and the importance of developing an entrepreneurial spirit. Most anyone who has achieved great success will tell you that they did so by becoming their own boss. It's an arduous task to develop true wealth while working a 9-5 job making someone else money.

To have an entrepreneurial spirit you have to think and live outside of the box. Always look for opportunities in your life to make money in unexpected ways. In order to achieve financial success you must plan to work longer than 9-5 and without a 'time clock' mentality. Stretch your definition of what it means to earn a living. Expand the parameters of how you can earn your living. Diversify the avenues in which money comes to you so that in an economic downturn in one particular industry, you still have other avenues and resources for earning money and/or making your money earn money for you.

I don't care what anyone says, being financially secure is not a bad thing. And remember you don't pay the price for success; you enjoy the price for success. You pay the price for failure.

I'm still living my dreams, still earning my own way, and still in a continual pattern of re-inventing myself when obstacles arise. I will always seek to find creative and innovative ways to be successful and accomplish my dreams and goals. The major difference between the early days and now? The cost of my toys has gone up considerably. Cars, motorcycles, musical instruments and recording equipment all tend to have large price tags and are hardly considered essential expenses for average daily living. But who wants to settle for average when you can achieve so much more?

I learned a long time ago that winners do what losers won't. I knew I had to work harder, smarter and more strategically to overcome my shortcomings of having dyslexia, of not being born to a family of privilege and having overcome health challenges early in life to ensure I had a chance to accomplish my dreams. I knew no one was going to hand me an opportunity; I had to go out there and create opportunities for myself and earn my way to where I wanted to be.

Be kind, for everyone you meet is
fighting a hard battle.

I'd like to say a word about a character trait I find integral to being a successful person, and that is kindness. During my eight miserable months of being homeless and living on the streets of Hollywood, striving every day not just to find a way to work my way out of the desperate situation I had found myself in, but merely survive and eat each day, I experienced moments of overwhelmingly selfless human kindness. Moments that have stayed with me throughout my life and have inspired me to share love and selfless kindness when I can to those who cross my path.

I will never forget a woman named Ketty. I was so painfully broke and underfed that my weight had dropped a good 30 pounds. One day, Ketty brought me two sandwiches. I never knew bologna could taste like filet mignon, but I do now. That memory is part of what continues to drive me forward: remembering Ketty's kindness and how delicious something so simple can be. There were a few other angels I encountered during that journey who probably saved my life. Some with advice or an encouraging word, some with food, others with temporary shelter.

A life filled with loving deeds and good character is the best tombstone. Those who you inspired and shared your love with will remember how you made them feel long after your time has expired. So carve your name on hearts, not stone. What you have done for yourself alone dies with you; what you have done for others and the world remains for all time.

The most I can do for my friend is
simply be his friend.

In learning to think 'success' it bears remembering that you are what you think. How you think determines everything about how you act and express yourself. The way you act determines how others react to you. Your appearance reflects your confidence level, and your confidence level affects your ability to be successful.

Just as your appearance and confidence level influence other people, they also influence you. When you are looking your best, you feel your best and most confident. Talk to yourself positively. Tell yourself over and over again that you are important, you are likeable and capable, you will be successful at whatever you endeavor to achieve. Through practice and repetition you can train your mind to believe exactly that. It will be much easier to look into a mirror and say these things to yourself if you look the part and feel the part.

Have faith in your abilities! Without a humble, but reasonable, confidence in your own powers you cannot be successful or happy.

Some people have a tendency to believe that investing in your physical appearance makes you superficial. That's not at all what this concept is about. Don't you enjoy the way you feel on the inside when you leave the hair salon with a fresh new hairstyle, or even just a trim? Don't you enjoy the feeling of being complimented on a new outfit or shoes? The cost is not what's important. This is not about spending a fortune or the perceived status from the label on your clothes. The point is the priceless effect that simple outward changes have on your positive mental attitude.

Let's be honest here: the truth is that it's rather difficult to have a positive attitude and mindset of being a successful and self-confident woman when your hair is dirty and in a scrunchy on top of your head while you tool around your house in your sweats and a t-shirt all day. Or for men, when you haven't had a shave in a few days and you hang out all day in your sweaty workout gear.

The seemingly simplistic details of your outward physical appearance are in fact crucial to your success and well-being. It is imperative for you to look your best on the outside to project the success you want to achieve. If you look successful, carry yourself like a successful person and project confidence and success on the outside, it will go a long way toward achieving the success you desire.

Improving the quality of your life and creating a personal environment for success begins at a cellular level. If the bloodstream is filled with waste products, the resulting environment does not promote a strong, vibrant, healthy cell-life or biochemistry capable of creating a balanced emotional life for an individual. Small changes begin to make big impacts when building upon other changes.

The higher your energy level, the more efficient your body. The more efficient your body, the better you feel, and the more you will use your talent to produce outstanding results.

As you begin to achieve success and enjoy the changes in your world you must remember to not become egotistical. Keeping your attitude in check is a critical factor for true success. You will always need other people in your life, so learn to cultivate a likeable and confident person within yourself. And remember that another key element for success is striving to always achieve a level of inner peace.

The following are key elements for achieving a likeable and confident person within yourself:

- Learn to remember the names of the people you meet.
- Be comfortable with yourself... therefore comfortable with others.
- There is no one else in this world quite like you... therefore, be the best you that you can possibly be.
- Do your best to maintain a relaxed and easygoing temperament so your mind will stay open to *'think positive.'*
- Truly listen to other people and be ready to accept responsibility for your reactions towards them.
- Practice liking people until you get it right! Start by finding something you like about them. This means finding and focusing on any positive attributes they possess... not their negatives.

- Always acknowledge people's achievements and offer altruistic sympathy when required. Be honest, warm and open.
- Give your strength to others and they will give you genuine affection back.
- *E-G-O = Edging God Out! There is no room for ego in success.*

If you have nothing to be grateful for,
check your pulse.

I am at a stage in my life where I choose to help others live the dream that I once lived. I derive great joy and inner peace from coaching, training and mentoring young talent as they pursue their dreams. The joy I receive when I hear of their accomplishments is immeasurable and makes my spirit come alive.

I know I wouldn't be where I am today without assistance from others. I am humbled every day when I look back on my life and remember those who helped me along the way when they didn't have to. Those who had nothing to gain other than the peace in their own spirit that they helped someone else when they were in need. However, I made sure these people all knew one thing through their encounter with me: I wasn't looking for a free hand-out. I was looking for a way out. I was looking for any and every opportunity I could to make things better for myself.

I am a firm believer in the spiritual teachings: "God helps those who help themselves," and "If you give a man a fish, you feed him for a day; if you teach him how to fish, he'll eat for a lifetime."

> The greatest discovery of all time is that a person can change his future by merely changing his attitude.

CHAPTER EIGHT

Coming Full Circle

"The true standard of measurement for extraordinary outcomes is that which brings extraordinary benefits and fulfillment to me and the lives of others. That's success!"

—Steven K. Scott

Right now I am living the most recent reinvention of myself and my career: I teach, train, coach, mentor and manage talent. I work with established entertainers, aspiring entertainers and coach business professionals from numerous and varied different industries. I am living proof that if you're open to the opportunities that come your way, the possibilities for re-invention are virtually limitless—at any time and at any age.

My new calling began about ten years ago when I was asked to speak at a singing and dancing academy in San Diego, California. I was still in corporate banking at the time, so it was fun to tap back in to my creative side and reconnect with my passion for the arts. This one-time speaking engagement led to others at different acting academies around Los Angeles and San Diego. Little did I know at the time that things were lining up for me to be prepared to re-invent myself for a new career path after the collapse of the banking and real estate industries put an end to the path I was on.

As anyone who truly knows me will tell you, I have a heart for children. I love how open they are, how in touch with their dreams they still are. I especially have a soft spot for those with a passion for the arts. I love to share my knowledge and experience to help them achieve their own dreams of success in Hollywood. This new career trajectory was tailor-made for me and led to more projects than I could have initially imagined; and also led to many people coming in to my life that have truly blessed and enhanced it beyond measure. This career has afforded me not only the opportunity to share my years of experience in the creative arts fields of acting, dancing and singing; but also to guide and develop careers in the most arduous and unpredictable industry in the world.

Since I have yet to be blessed with children of my own, it is a true gift in my life to be able to pour my energies into the many amazingly creative kids I have had the privilege to teach, train, mentor and coach. Then there are the precious few that have crossed over into the realm of being my management clients. But just like with parenting, the joys and triumphs can often come with some major heartbreaks and disappointments.

I frequently get asked "What do you do?" "What is an acting coach?" or "What does a manager do?" Sometimes it's best to explain by sharing personal examples, so here are a few brief summaries of the careers of some of the talent I have developed as a manager. Because the management of a young person's career is so intensely personal, and I become so deeply connected and involved, I have chosen to keep my roster of management clients down to a precious few compared to other managers in the industry. Not that my way is better than anyone else's or to say other managers aren't really fantastic at what they do for their clients, this is just what feels right for me as my personal style of working: All passion. All in. All the time.

The quality of your life is the
quality of your relationships.

James Maslow

I was just getting my feet wet again in the entertainment industry as a guest speaker at established acting schools. One particular lecture I gave was in San Diego and that day an average-looking, pimply-faced kid approached me after class and asked what it would take to become a successful actor/singer. During our conversation, I noticed he had a tangible spark when he spoke about performing. I quickly realized that this was the type of kid I wanted to work with. His tenacity, ambition and innate talents were immediately apparent and traits I knew I would love to develop.

BILLY AND JAMES MASLOW

I knew James had the potential for both a television career and a successful music career, so I set about devising the backwards plan to develop a career to accomplish the defined goals and objectives. Initially I told him he would have to attend multiple classes—virtually every day of the week—to develop the skills and discipline necessary to start on the path to success. In addition to enhancing his performance skills, I advised the kid that he would also need to focus on his health and fitness, as both have a huge impact on personal appearance. Finally, if we were going to work together, he would have to listen to everything I advised him to do and be humble all the while, because the entertainment industry is unlike any other. As an acting coach, my goal was to guide and mentor James to develop his creative talents and abilities to the highest level possible. Additionally, my goal was to educate him on every aspect of how to get a job and sustain a career in Hollywood.

Over the course of the next several years this young man persevered, overcame his own personal obstacles and worked very hard studying different aspects of his craft (acting, singing and dancing) every day. He was cast in several small parts along the way. Then he had an opportunity to audition for an upcoming pilot project for Nickelodeon that utilized all of his skills. After two years of auditioning for the same one role, his patience and perseverance finally paid off. James Maslow was placed under contract for the role of James Diamond in *Big Time Rush.* This single opportunity caused him to become an international household name.

With this new role my job as coach to James transitioned into personal manager. As a manager guiding his career, it became my responsibility to advise him and direct every aspect of his career—from reading scripts to ensuring the right publicity, personal appearances, endorsements and additional projects were aligned with the primary strategic objectives for the future development of his career.

Early on, James had declared his goals were to get on a television series and to have a record deal. One day, when he was well-established on *Big Time Rush* and had put out an album, he and I were driving up the hill to my house. He looked at me and said, "Remember my goal? To get a TV series and a record deal? That has happened. Thank you." Mission: Impossible had become Mission Accomplished.

To put his accomplishments in perspective, at the same time that some of James' high school classmates were graduating from college to begin their careers with over $100,000 in debt hanging over their heads, James had already earned well over a million dollars and had toured around the world. As arduous as the entertainment industry is and as unpredictable as to if and when you will receive that "yes" that will change your life forever, this is also one of the few industries where you can become financially independent in a very short amount of time.

I am so proud of all of James' success and accomplishments and could not have been more thrilled to watch him compete so fiercely each week on *"Dancing with the Stars."* He will always hold a special place in my heart as he was my first client to fully train and develop from an average kid with big dreams, to watching his dreams come true right before my eyes.

Ciara Hanna

Ciara Hanna

With any growing business, you network to create new contacts and re-connect with those you once knew in the trenches, when you were all in the beginning of your careers. In the entertainment industry, this usually equates to the catering assistant or production intern from twenty years ago now holding an executive-level position. That's one of the key reasons I always advise people to be kind and respectful to people at every level of this industry; you just never know where they'll be in another decade or two. You certainly always want everyone to remember you kindly.

One day I received a phone call from an agent friend who thought her client could benefit from coaching and training in my classes. She advised me that this particular client was stunningly beautiful so she was always getting her in the door to be seen by casting directors. Even with the advantage of her looks, she was having challenges booking jobs. This isn't an uncommon challenge for actors to overcome, so I said I would love to meet her to see if we could work together.

Ciara and I had a great rapport. After a few coaching sessions I intuitively knew that if I took her on as a management client I could set in motion a backwards plan for her to achieve her dream of booking a television series and begin on a path of becoming a successful actor.

After some intensive coaching, Ciara broke through her internal mental barriers and booked a recurring role on the daytime series *The Bold and The Beautiful.* This one *yes* increased her confidence level, her acting abilities and her level of performance delivery. Several commercials and guest star appearances followed before she booked a starring role on Nickelodeon's *Power Rangers Mega Force,* which took her to the exotic locale of New Zealand for eight months of filming. Ciara followed that success with booking two feature films, including one shot on location in Bangkok, Thailand.

I believe Ciara has the confidence and acting abilities to book any job she sets her mind to if she's right for the role.

Jake Short

BILLY AND JAKE SHORT

As my management career continued to grow, along with growing my acting classes and coaching business, I continued to speak at various acting seminars filled with young hopefuls. At one of these events I had the pleasure of meeting Jake Short, an established actor who was successfully working on the Disney series *A.N.T. Farm.* I was pleased when he chose to begin taking acting classes and private coaching with me to further enhance his talents and skills.

Over time, my coaching evolved into assisting him with the development of a more unified social media presence, website and expansion of his identity/name recognition as an actual marketing brand. And not long after that, he asked me to become his manager, assisting in further developing his career and taking things to the next level. Since Jake was already an established actor on a television series, the strategy for his career development was a little bit different. The plan developed for him entailed establishing a solid brand identity, building his fan base and insuring he didn't get type cast in the role on a children's series he was known for but transitioning him into more mature roles.

As with any new venture, the social media development was initially slow, yet within a year's time Jake's social media following on Facebook alone increased from 77,913 likes (February 2013) to just under 3.2 million (May 2014) and increases exponentially every day.

While still filming *A.N.T. Farm,* Jake had several great opportunities to audition for pilots during the 2013 pilot season. Pilot season is historically a 3-4 month time frame at the beginning of each new year where all of the major networks look at potential new shows that they are either developing themselves or that other production companies are producing in hopes that a major network will pick them up for their fall line-up. I say historically, because with so many cable networks and new media opportunities available, this traditional structure is quickly becoming a thing of the past as pilots are cast throughout the year.

In preparation for one of his auditions, Jake proved why my instincts were right—that this was another special young talent I could wholeheartedly pour myself and talents into, professionally speaking. After doing his own due diligence by memorizing his lines, finding the appropriate emotions and understanding his character, he arrived ready for a coaching session specifically centered on preparation for this one audition. We spent two and a half hours working, reworking, stretching, challenging and developing his character through repeatedly performing the same five-page scene over and over and over again.

Finally, we felt he was 100% prepared for the audition the next day. Throughout this process it was crucial that I tap into different emotions and character connections so that when Jake had his appointment with the casting directors, they wouldn't only see elements of Fletcher Quimby, the character Jake was actively playing every day on the set of *A.N.T. Farm.*

Jake proved then, and has repeatedly proven since, that he has the drive, determination, tenacity, fortitude and positive personal character traits that it takes to be truly successful at anything in life, Hollywood included. His audition was a huge success. He not only booked the pilot but his series was also picked up for a permanent slot on Disney XD's network.

And better still, Disney announced that the series *Mighty Med* will be picked up for a second season. Great things continue to unfold in the life and career of this talented young actor.

Tenzing Norgay Trainor

TENZING WITH GARY MARSHALL

Tenzing came to me by way of an agent referral, not unlike Ciara. The conversation went something like this:

Agent: "I've got this kid. He has something interesting and cool about him, but he's inexperienced and going to need a lot of work. I think he's going to need to coach with you for at least a year before he's ready to start really going out on auditions. Let me know how it goes. I'm sure I'll see him again in about a year."

Me: "Um, OK."

When Tenzing showed up for his first class with me, I immediately picked up on his overwhelming desire and determination to succeed. Although he was a somewhat reserved and quiet child, when he stepped up to perform his scene, something magical occurred that I was the only one to see. I knew this kid had something truly special, because the characters he conveyed through delivery of a scene came to life. His performance style was to give 200%. Then he would humbly walk back to his seat, prepared to intently watch his fellow students' performances.

After meeting with his dad and arranging an intensive training program, Tenzing took group classes or private coaching every week. At the tender age of ten, he was able to tap into the intensive discipline he had honed through years of martial arts training to work tirelessly toward his goal of becoming a successful working actor in Hollywood.

After just five weeks of this rigorous training program, I once again had a conversation with the original referring agent that went something like this:

Me: "Remember that boy you sent to me five weeks ago to take classes… you thought he might need a year of training before he's ready?"

Agent: "Yes."

Me: "He's ready. This kid is a monster."

Agent: "What? No way. I'll see him again in a year. Maybe six months."

Me: "Seriously? If you don't want to meet with him again, that's fine—but I know you'll be kicking yourself for missing this opportunity because my next call will be to another agent. He's ready."

Agent: "Um, OK."

At their next meeting, she signed him on the spot. Tenzing went on to land guest-starring roles on multiple shows, complete two movies and become a star on one of Disney's most successful new series, *Liv and Maddie.* By the time he was twelve years old. Tenzing has accomplished so much in his young life thanks to his drive, dedication, perseverance and tenacity. My personal goal was to make him a million dollars before he was fifteen years old. He's well on his way!

So Much Talent/So Many Dreams

Since starting down this path of teaching, training, motivating and sometimes even managing young talent, I have had the unique pleasure of working with thousands of actors, actresses, singers and dancers. I have coached young and old alike sharing the skills, techniques, tips and insight that were acquired over three decades of successful experience in the entertainment industry. I am delighted to have assisted talent in booking more than 180 different (and counting) commercials, television series, feature films and pilots throughout the time I have been on the other side of the camera in this business.

In addition to the four I just mentioned, I have been privileged to coach and train many successful, recognizable talents. This is a brief partial list of notable clients:

Amanda Leighton

Make it or Break it

90210

The Young and the Restless

The Fosters

Daniela Bobadilla

Awake

Anger Management

Shyann McClure

National Welch's Grape Juice Campaign

Premonition

House, M.D.

Mackenzie Foy

Twilight: Breaking Dawn I & II

Olivia Holt

Kickin It

Girl vs. Monster

I Didn't Do it!

Audrey Whitby

Bad Fairy

So Random

Austin & Ally

Olivia Stuck

Kirby Buckets

Last Vegas

Girl Meets World

Although the list of clients I have entered into management agreements with is small, I have been privileged to be coach and train many equally talented or magical performers. It's just that for whatever reason—circumstances with life and/or business—certain coaching relationships seemed to inherently develop to the management level while others didn't. It's very true when people talk about "Right Place/Right Time." Oftentimes success is just that simple.

Olivia Holt and Jake Short at Radio Disney Music Awards

Billy and Eryn Pablico

Raising Asia

BILLY AND ASIA MONET RAY

Recently, at a time when I was contemplating dissolving my management company because of intensely personal separations with two of my oldest clients, I had the opportunity to meet the talented Miss Asia Monet Ray, an eight-year-old dance phenomenon with larger-than-life career aspirations. This half-African-American/half-Filipino firecracker was ready to take on the entertainment world. I felt an immediate connection to Asia and soon developed a strong and close bond with she and her family.

Asia had achieved success prior to entering my life. She is an undefeated international dance champion who, at the age of six, booked recurring roles on two different Lifetime network reality series: *Abby's Ultimate Dance Competition* and *Dance Moms,* in which both she and her mom appeared.

Initially, I was approached to be Asia's vocal and acting coach. Prior to my meeting, I later discovered two different entertainment managers had approached Asia's mom looking to represent her daughter. Each of them had recommended two other vocal coaches. After our initial meeting, we both knew that Asia and I working together was a match. She and I had a strong immediate connection because of our shared dance background. Before agreeing to represent an eight-year-old, I let her know how difficult a task this was going to be. I stated clearly that the success she wanted to achieve might not happen for quite some time. Asia asked me, "What does that mean?" and I responded, "Years." Her immediate response was "Let's do it!" I knew then that my instincts about her were correct: she had the drive and perseverance to accomplish her dreams.

Out of professional courtesy, I contacted the two managers who had previously approached Asia's mom, Kristie, to see if they were okay with my managing her. They gave their blessings, and we were off. Asia amazed me in that as an eight-year-old, she was willing to invest the necessary time in training and coaching. As a coach, I can always tell when someone is working on their own time, between coaching sessions. With me, a student can't just dial it in. I can hear if they're doing the work on their own time, whether the work is acting or singing. I can always immediately tell who is investing their personal time in developing their careers and who isn't taking it quite as seriously.

Asia possessed both the desire and wholehearted commitment. She trained for hours and hours a day, not because her parents make her but because she chooses to. She never wanted to stop training. At the age of only eight, it's amazing that this young girl understands the vital importance of dedicating herself to daily intensive study and training.

Throughout the process of developing a strategy for accomplishing the backwards plan of achieving the goals set out, I was repeatedly told I was nuts to think I could sell an eight- year-old. I was told it would be next to impossible to get her on TV or to get her a record deal. People do not typically buy music from an artist that young. No one that young has ever had a hugely successful music career since Michael Jackson.

After a few short months of working together and maintaining a rigorous training schedule, I not only helped negotiate the Lifetime television deal *Raising Asia* but I also negotiated a recording contract with Neon Pink Records. And I just booked her in a role in the feature film "Sista Code." Again: Persistence Breaks Resistance. Remember when someone says you can't do something, know that you can.

The reality show for Lifetime was a show of her own, completely centered on her life, with her name in the title: *Raising Asia.* I had accomplished what so many others had deemed impossible, and in a very short amount of time. I confidently, but humbly, predicted that I would get her on television and develop her music career. Both have come to fruition.

As a result of my young client's reality series, I was pulled back into the world of reality television—this time from a completely different angle. Furthermore, managing someone on a reality show is a completely different world from managing an actor on a scripted television series. It's a very unpredictable, demanding and time consuming task.

GINA SAMERIO I really didn't know who Billy Hufsey was. Of course once I met him I remembered him from FAME and so forth, but my sister Kristie had been talking about him as my niece Asia's coach/manager. We were introduced on the set of Dance Moms one day and started chatting. He told me that he was going to turn Asia into a singer. Now, I am very close to Asia, and I had heard her sing. I had some serious reservations. I know with Asia's level of talent for dance, she can get up onstage and wing anything. But singing? That's a whole different talent. When he said he could turn Asia into a singer in a couple of months, I frankly thought he was delusional. My first thought was, Who do you think you are? Who was this man who had just come into my niece's life to tell me what my niece was capable of? Me, who knew her inside and out?

I knew that putting Asia up onstage to sing when she wasn't prepared would be devastating to her. That kid is an absolute perfectionist and when she messes up a dance routine she is crying and inconsolable for hours. I did not want her hurt by trying something in public that she was not well-trained in. Billy had only known Asia for a month or two at that time... I'd known her since the day she was born!

Throughout Asia's life I was often the one in the audience watching her performances, because my sister had to be backstage with her. I would see everyone else perform and be able to tell Kristie and Asia how all the other young dancers had done that day. I have watched Asia perform hundreds of times; I feel I know exactly what she can and cannot do. I just did not see singing in her future. I'd heard her sing an Alicia Keys song once and couldn't help but laugh. It was honestly kind of sweet... because Asia thought she sounded great. In my humble opinion, she needed to stick with dancing. Oh, and lose the big bows on her head... that's just an aunt's opinion!

I have to say that I have never been more wrong. That girl can sing. With Billy's help, my niece will be famous, because she can truly sing now. I am her biggest critic, and I am willing to be brutally honest with her. I will be the first to tell her she sounds too nasally or is trying too hard to sound like someone she's not. The first time I saw her up on stage singing, I cried. The tears literally rolled down my face. It was magical!

I doubted Billy, and he proved me wrong. Billy managed to bring out her own true voice and turn her into a beautiful and accomplished singer. When I see them working together, their close connection is so obvious. Without Billy, there is no way she would be all that she is today. I would not have believed this could happen if I hadn't seen it with my own eyes... or, more importantly, heard it with my own ears! I have never been so happy to be wrong!

Another Dose of Reality

As we all know by now, the goal of reality television is to get unscripted drama on camera through the viewing of everyday life. The goal of producers in reality television is to get as much drama packed into as few as possible days of filming to keep expenses low. The reality of filming a show completely centered around the life of an eight-year-old translates to shorter workdays due to California labor laws governing children in the entertainment industry. What does all of this mean? It means that the producers often scheduled Asia to perform with little to no preparation or rehearsal time.

Her parents and I had to fight to get Asia this time—paramount for a dancer who performs at her level. Not only does she require time to properly warm up to give the level of performance her fans and audiences have come to expect from her—let alone what she expects from herself—we also have to always be cognizant of her safety. She must be properly warmed up and stretched out. She must have time to familiarize herself with the venue in which she is performing. There are many surfaces that could not only be detrimental to Asia but could potentially cause permanent damage to her still developing child's body.

Early on the producers of the show asked me to step in front of the camera for one episode as a prospective manager for Asia. They wanted to capture that relationship on film for story-line continuity. After my first day of filming, the producers asked that I continue my role on the show. Although I had no desire to be a regular, I decided to concede as it would help Asia, which was then, and always has been, my sole focus throughout this project.

While a reality show is supposed to film your daily life from afar, the reality of reality is that it eventually consumes everything you do. Therein lies a certain irony of Reality TV. That's what began to happen to me: I was being consumed. I was working so hard doing double duty that I got sick... very, very sick. I was working on the show in front of the cameras, working diligently behind the scenes developing Asia's music, managing her other career opportunities, continuing to coach and develop her creative talents all while still managing to maintain management of my other clients' careers, keep up with acting classes and private coaching sessions, as well as oversee several other companies I own. Needless to say, eventually I was put on bed rest for two days, and then was taken to a hospital. Even then, I remained completely committed to the project and resumed work the same day I left the hospital.

Any sacrifices on my part have all been worth it to see Asia succeed—for her dreams are my passions, and when she succeeds, my passions are fulfilled. The same holds true for my other management clients. When they accomplish their dreams and the goals they have worked hard to achieve, my heart is full.

The Next Re-Invention

I have often said that true success comes from either inspiration or desperation. As no one in the traditional recording industry had the slightest desire to sign an eight-year-old to a recording contract—let alone one who had only been professionally training as a singer for a very short time as Asia had—I was inspired. I had been told by half-a-dozen of the top industry professionals that it was impossible to make a half African-American, half-Filipino child dancer into a star when she had previously never sung or acted in her life. So I responded to my own need to fulfill Asia's dreams of becoming the next Beyonce by assembling a team to work with me to produce and write the songs for Asia's record.

This assembled team will now provide a platform and incalculable opportunities to develop additional projects and creative ventures for my other management clients in addition to all of the exciting projects being developed for Asia. The wheels of creativity are just beginning to spin for all of the exciting potential and possibilities to come.

At a time when I was seriously contemplating walking away from the most recent career re-invention I had created for myself, a tiny eight-year-old, highly motivated, creative powerhouse walked into my life to become a breath of fresh air, reinvigorating my desire to do what I do now: Help others to live the dream I once lived.

KRISTIE RAY My daughter Asia became well-known when she was featured on the popular reality show Dance Moms. The producers started talking about offering Asia her own show during the very first season, when she was only seven years old. I encouraged her to spend another year on Dance Moms, so she could get a bit older and more mature. We could both learn more about the whole reality world and what it would entail if she starred in her own show. Asia had a great run on Dance Moms, but after two seasons there was nothing left for her to do. It was time for her to go.

We were at a crossroads. Asia had some management companies interested in representing her, but none of them were capable of taking her to the level we were hoping to achieve. There was a lot of talk about her being the next Hannah Montana, because of her unique style and personality, but that was going to be a reach. It's difficult to cross over in the entertainment world from dancer to singer and actor and be accepted. It's also hard to get someone to believe and focus on other talents, because Asia was only known as a brilliant young dancer. That's all most people wanted her to do, because she's very good at it. We needed to find just the right person; someone who really saw all of her potential.

One of these potential managers said, "Let's focus on her vocals. I'm going to give you two names. The first is a good solid vocal coach who has worked with a number of young artists. The second guy, Billy Hufsey, comes from a dance background himself. I think Asia might really connect with him; he's very animated and hyper like Asia. I have a feeling they'll hit it off."

The very first time they met, it was immediately clear that Billy and Asia were two peas in a pod. Their stories were so similar; there was such an instantaneous great connection. Given their shared dance background, I think Billy saw a lot of himself in my daughter. Even better, Billy absolutely, completely believed in her potential as a singer. The two of us discussed the future. I explained to Billy that we were kind of going back and forth about doing this proposed new reality show.

"What does Asia really want to do?" Billy asked me.

I said, "I think she really wants to act and sing."

"So, for the time being, let's focus on that," he said. And the two of them began an intensive coaching schedule, three days a week. Asia's progress was simply remarkable. She was progressing by leaps and bounds; very soon she was becoming a genuine triple threat dancer / singer / actor. Billy was absolutely instrumental in that growth.

Soon enough Billy walked my daughter right into the office of one of the biggest agents in Hollywood. These people weren't even aware that Asia was a veteran of two TV dance shows. Billy had prepared her well. "You will be reading these five pages of script. You are going to sell yourself as an actress." Now, Asia always rises to the occasion, but walking into

Paradigm to audition as an actress was a high-stakes move. She was anxious to prove to Billy that she could indeed do this; that his faith in her was justified. Any audition is always a bit iffy with an 8-year-old; it's never guaranteed that they'll be able to focus long enough and deliver on demand. It was asking a lot for her to cross over from that hyper dancer energy to memorizing lines and performing dramatically. I was more nervous than Asia! But sure enough… she performed beautifully that day. She was off and running!

"Billy," I said, "we have a decision to make. The producers really want to give Asia her own show. Is the timing right?" I was really worried about taping a reality show and its repercussions for Asia's long-term prospects. Would she be able to cross over later as a character on a Disney or Nickelodeon show?

"You can't deny talent," Billy told me. "If there's a problem, her talent will still always be undeniable." Her new agent at Paradigm and Billy agreed that we should proceed with a new reality show: Raising Asia. It was a great opportunity to give Asia the platform of her name on her own show, featuring a young girl's journey to becoming a true artist: an actor/dancer/singer.

Asia adores Billy; no matter what's going on, Billy always brings the calm to her. I really needed someone like that in our lives; I needed not to be the momager anymore. I wanted to just be Asia's mom; I'd been handling her dance stuff since she was two years old, and enough was enough. It was time for me to step back. I was willing to hand over that control because I trust so much in Billy and his judgment.

Since Billy came into our lives everything has changed. Asia has a separate relationship with Billy where she can confide in him, and the two of us are parent and child again... which was missing for most of her life. Not to mention, I also have another child! I am so happy to be just plain MOM again! The more I was around Billy the surer I was that I made the best decision.

Billy is a passionate workaholic who won't take no for an answer—if you tell him he can't do something, he'll run right out to do it. I had a number of professionals tell me flat-out, "You cannot turn this child dancer into a star. You won't be able to find her an agent." That was the first thing he set out to do... and he did it. That's just Billy! Billy is that type of person, which makes for a great manager. He transfers his personal stamina and drive and never-say-no energy over to his kids. And they all perform at their peaks, because Billy ensures that they do. They want to please him.

He gives this same energy to all his clients, not just Asia. He only takes on a few, but when he believes in someone, he gives it his all. Anyone who is lucky enough to get Billy to take them on has his undivided attention. The man does not sleep. I'm a mom, so I don't sleep, but he really doesn't sleep! Another plus is that Billy's not a yes guy, he's real. He'll tell you straight out what needs to be said. When I ask him something, he will tell me the unvarnished truth. Some moms don't like that; they don't want to hear something even slightly negative about their child, but I appreciate his honesty. You're in the wrong business if you can't take the truth. I trust his instincts a hundred percent.

So on the reality show Raising Asia, Billy was supposed to be a Charlie's Angels sort of figure... an unseen voice on the phone as "the manager"—which quickly morphed into him appearing in every episode. The performer Billy was back on camera!

At the end of the day Billy is a good person with a good heart who does a great job bringing out the best in Asia. Who else would I trust with my child?

Final Thoughts

"A single dream is more powerful than a thousand realities."
—J.R.R. Tolkien

A Full Circle Moment

A year or so ago, as I was in the beginning stages of working on this book, I experienced what I consider to be a God moment. A moment where your past comes full circle and you are granted the opportunity to acknowledge somebody or something who was responsible for the positive direction your life took or some success you've achieved. These moments are a rare gift indeed, and I am blessed that I was open and ready for the encounter.

I was walking into Jerry's Deli on Ventura Boulevard in Tarzana, California when I passed an elderly man who looked somewhat familiar to me. My initial thought was of my own elderly dad back home in Cleveland, Ohio, so I instinctively smiled with kindness and understanding. When our eyes locked I had a moment of clarity. Recognition shot through me like a jolt. "Bill? Is that you?" I asked. He responded with a simple "Yeah."

I couldn't suppress the huge smile that came straight from my heart and spirit at this fortuitous encounter. I told him, "I am so happy and fulfilled at this moment, and want to say thank you." His blunt response made me smile even bigger. "What for?"

My heart swelled as I replied, "You took a chance when I was living on the streets and hired me."

Recognition dawned on his face as he questioned, "Billy Hufsey?" All I could do was nod and reply with a simple, "Yes." Now I was blessed to see the answering smile on his face as he replied, "I am so grateful for this moment. You gave us everything we expected—and then some. Thank *you!*"

This chance encounter was with Bill Blenn, producer of *Fame* and the key decision-maker who chose to hire me for the role of *Christopher Donlon,* when the 40,000 original applicants were narrowed down to four. I have to admit there were tears in my eyes as I gave him a big hug. I knew I would probably never have an opportunity to see him again. What a blessed moment that was!

Sometimes on life's journey, you forget the person who said "Yes!" and changed your life. Sometimes it's easy to forget where you've come from when you're touring around the world on private planes with hundreds of thousands of fans screaming your name. I was beyond blessed to be a part of a ground-breaking show that not only changed my life personally, but also changed the world.

Bill Blenn believed in me and chose me over the other extremely talented actors who had far more credits than I at the time. He saw something in me of what I could bring to the role. He gave me the first "Yes!" that forever changed my life. As I often tell my students, it only takes one yes to change your world. I know, because it happened for me, so I know it can happen for them. May it happen for you as well!

The man who keeps busy helping the man below him won't have time to envy the man above him.

As an entertainer myself, there's no greater joy than knowing I'm putting smiles on faces and in the hearts of my audience. As an entertainment coach, there's no greater joy than achieving my goal to help my students achieve their highest level of performance ability and experience.

As a manager, there's no greater joy than guiding a client's career so that they can put smiles on faces through multiple projects and entertainment platforms over the course of a long-standing sustainable career. There's no other way I would rather spend my time on this earth.

> The way we communicate with others, and with ourselves, ultimately determines the quality of our lives.

One thing I know for sure is that no one is going to live forever; there's only one way out of this world. I personally plan on living life to its fullest until my last breath. I have always loved the famous Hunter S. Thompson quote about dying: "Life should not be a journey to the grave with the intention of arriving safely in a well-preserved body, but rather to skid in broadside in a cloud of smoke, thoroughly used up, totally worn out, and loudly proclaiming 'Wow! What a ride!'"

You have to live each and every day to its fullest because once it's gone, you can never get it back. We always hear people say things like, "If I knew I had a year left to live I would…" or ponder "What would you change in your daily life if you knew you only had a certain amount of time left to live?" I don't want to get to my last days of life with any regrets or lingering questions about *should have, would have, could have*. Life is not a dress rehearsal!

We're not here for a long time, but a good time, so make it the best life you possibly can by following the dreams and passions in your heart. If you take nothing else from this book please remember, God doesn't put dreams in your heart without giving you the ability to achieve them!

15441154R00117

Made in the USA
San Bernardino, CA
26 September 2014